THE NOOSE ON THE BLACK COMMUNITY

THE NOOSE ON THE BLACK COMMUNITY

CHRISTOPHER SULLIVAN

CONTENTS

Author's Note

My greatest gratitude is towards God and my family for their unwavering support secondary to the amount of time spent working on this book. My three sons Christopher Jr., Rashad, and Chad have been very instrumental in the completion of this book. I have looked upon their faces many days and wondered, what is it that I can do today to make being a good father the ultimate experience, and then I breathe a sigh of relief for my active presence in their lives.

I would also like to thank the many friends that believed in me, even when I was starting to second guess myself. Throughout this ordeal I have come to realize that hope is that experience that never fades, and if you feel like hope is seen, then you must close your eyes and rely on the things that are unseen...For they are infinite.

Last but not least, I want to thank my wife Sandee for her unwavering support. She has been a ray of sunshine down to the inner core of my being. Thank you for being my wife, friend, and listener, during the times I worked on this project. Without your patience and understanding, my work will be incomplete.

The Noose on the Black Community

The tragic truth behind the present day killing of black youths in America and those responsible for the continued downfall of the black community.

Introduction

For a number of years now, I often wonder why we as black males respond to each other much differently than we do other males. When I read the papers about youths being killed in America, it is usually a black male killing another black male. When I look at the news concerning arm robbery, shootings, or home invasions, it is usually black on black crime that occurs and without failure those that are aware of the crime oftentimes refuse to snitch.

Through the years and from experience, I realize that if I am going to defend myself against anyone in this world it would be me defending myself against another black male. This is troubling to me considering all the hardship that blacks have come through only to rise up against another black person that have shared similar struggles, stereotypes, and hardships. Even though I grew up in a predominantly black neighborhood, those difficult experiences of social suffering and black on black crime being played out on the same field was always difficult to comprehend.

One would think that those who suffer together the most would rise up and protect each other, especially if they are suffering for the same cause. I tried not to delve into the subject of this matter too deep, because after all, I am black and to bring about the exposure of how too many black males (especially) are acting is more than embarrassing.

However, as I grow older I now realize that the truth concerning my black brothers are very troublesome. The troublesome parts arise from how we treat each other, how we respect each other, and most of all the respect that we carry for ourselves on a daily basis.

These concerns call for a reevaluation not only of "self" but the reevaluation on how you as a black male may perceive the world around you, as well as the pathway to truth concerning victimization and black male bonding.

Like so many others, I have asked the question, what is going on with black males? It seems as if many of us can't get it together and anger has become the solution to resolve every conflict that is thrown at us. For such a group of men which derived from strong and mighty ancestors, it is certain that our present day fight has escalated into a war amongst ourselves.

Should we blame former slave masters of the past that drove black men into a state of uncertainty concerning their manhood? Should we blame the system that houses thousands of black males each year for the same old crime against their own kind? Should we blame the fathers of the males that displaced themselves from the family unit? Or should we blame ourselves for the unrecognized accountable acts we subject ourselves to, and the lack of good character we sometimes fail to produce?

With that being said, one must recognize those paralyzing agents that are before him, if one is to grow on the inside morally. Although there are many paralyzing agents that attach themselves to black males, it is when you take part and become a part of the experience that ultimately leads to destruction.

One of the biggest paralyzing agents in the black community for black males are drugs, and before this can be conquered, accountability must be understood.

With all fairness, if we really look at the crimes that occur amongst black males in the black communities, those responsible for the crimes committed are simply those that commit them, and this has cripple the black community in an unparalleled way.

Furthermore, what sometime appears to be an acceptable lifestyle in the black community can easily stop the upward social mobility of black families. This is done by confining black males to a lifestyle that will rarely create hope and prevent growth.

As a black man, I now realize that if you fail to recognize those negative issues surrounding you, then those same negative issues will become the noose that asphyxiate your thoughts and lifestyle. The noose I am speaking of is that psychological experience in which many black males entertain, and the negative actions use against each other for the reason of committing death and perpetrating love.

Finally, in recent years this Noose has resurfaced upon the minds of many black males, challenging their purpose, their morals, reasoning, and most of all the love for the family and community. Some may argue that the problem is not as big as the media creates it to be, but for those that feel that way I beg you to delve into the black community and notice the number of black males that are taking pleasure in hanging each other by selling drugs, robbing and committing murder. Then ask yourself, is there really a noose amongst the black community?

Who's Hanging Black Men Now?

"Dispersed throughout the fine parts of humility abides a sense of strengthening, which leaves hope to wonder, and little faith to hold onto. While these experiences of life is only for a moment, we must take pride in acknowledging the truth, and without it we would never discover our way....CS

The many issues that plague the black community are often overlooked by those none other than, black men within the community. The world stands as the audience while the continuation of young black men perpetuate the onslaught of black on black violence and continually destroy black communities. Moreover, it seems as if love can't be offered as a gift to stop the anger that is destroying a generation of black men, as some hold their culture hostage and look for others to blame.

One may ask, what is the problem? Usually when we witness random killings it involves the assailant(s) having mental issues or a personal problem that may have gotten out of control. But the only way to analyze and rectify the issues that are plaguing this black generation is to unveil the truth. The truth exist within the perimeters of the black mind and can be found in the corners of the streets in which many black males seek to control, but inadvertently destroy.

In reality, we have witnessed many scores of young black men pitch their anger against other black men, and this have depicted a curved angle that seems difficult to straighten out.

When young black youths kill each other, it is not a white fight, nor is it a fight against the system, as if the system itself is responsible for the continuation of black murders. But when we witness black men killing each other, we are witnessing a self destructive fight that starts with individual hatred and ends with the death of one black male who never tried to understand the life of another black man nor his own.

It is tragic to say that the number of black men murdered by other black men is more than ridiculous. During a period of 86 years, the KKK was responsible for perhaps a little over 3440 black murders in the United States. According to statistics the numbers of black males that kill others of the same race every 6-8 months in America are well over 3440. In other words, the number of black deaths cause by other black men makes what happened during the Jim Crow years seems innocent.

Needless to say, the very thought of opening up ones' mind to what really goes on in the streets of black America only arrest my hopes and desires to speak the truth and the truth is that black men are continuing to fall from their responsibilities and are being hung.

Along with this fall is the non accountability many black males never accept for the actions they implement. Too many black males strive to become drug dealers, but there is no accountability from the violence this incurs. Too many black males form community gangs that bring terror, but too few are willing to accept the dilapidation they cause their own living environment. Without acknowledging this painful truth, it will always falsify the path of direction that one takes, and the failure to realize the truth will never bring forth a true destination. It will always present a platform to blame.

Aside from this, if we as black males continue to lack the means to realize those issues standing before us, then our "once upon a time" victory will continue to dissipate into a valley of defeat, and this is what many blacks are witnessing today. In doing so, it will invite a lack of hope that will remain suppressed due to non-established knowledge, and an unwillingness to love one another along with a willingness to fight and kill the other.

Onward, the fate of young black men today is continuing to distant itself from the reach of a father's voice. If fathers can't lead with positivity, then how does the unit stands? Without redefining that of good and moral behavior, many more black males will not only implement a destructive lineage of spiritual strongholds to come, but it will seemingly wipe out the nuclear family of the black race.

So my question is where are you black man? Where do you hide? Where are the black fathers, and where are those that care enough to protect their families and their communities? Where are you, I ask? Where do you lie when black kids are being murdered in the streets? Where is your voice of concern and paddle of correction? Where do you hide while the drugs are being passed in front of our children faces? Where is your concern? Where do you go when the teens walk the streets as gangs and take ownership of the community at such young ages? Where are those parental skills that care enough to correct, and love enough to destroy the hate simmering in the minds of too many black males? So, where does longevity lie and when do black men take a stand?

If you were truthful about answering these questions you would understand the need for peace, and extend a hand of help to those that follow along the wrong pathways with a finite mind, and the inability to walk in a more decent way. Once this is understood, wisdom and peace will have its' way.

The abuse or killings that arise between black males within the U.S. is so overlooked by the black community, that it has become an acceptable way of life for many black families.

When a young black kid is killed on the streets, it seems to be accepted because it has become common place. When blacks rob and kill other black victims within the community, it's accepted. When people are shot at clubs, or home invasions occurs ending in the life of an innocent person, it is all accepted. The reasoning behind the acceptance is secondary to the weakness stemming from the community of black men who have forfeited their march on the black race and now deny themselves the "meaning of care" for the safety of black children and a focused driven community.

Having forfeited such an experience as this one has led to the blindness of truth which seems to encourage such tragedies, and a blind obedience with an obscured vision. But as usual, before people hit the streets with anti killing signs, there have to be a high number of murders before many blacks within the community will ever recognize it. This depicts a non concerned mind for the failing community and this ideal of being non expressive must be pushed aside. Without proactive experiences such as these, the suffocation of black males will continue to be seen and those to blame are only the "black man, and the black man only.

A Noose on the Mind

With the ongoing violence that we witness throughout the many cities in America, it is obvious that a large group of black American males are being asphyxiated. This asphyxiation occurs by what I consider to be the "Noose" upon the mind. This noose is found hanging in many black communities. In the past, when black males were being hung and slaughtered by an inconsiderate justice system, black men and women alike were the loudest to voice their opinions.

It was obvious that the hangings or castrations of any man secondary to the color of his skin was wrong, but blacks never laid down without voicing their opinions. Had not the many voices of Black Americans touched the soul of the people that had a heart, then the road to equality would have remained blocked. Had this happened, the blockage would have kept America's eyes closed to the truth of racism and the senseless murdering of black men would be the same as today.

At the other end of the spectrum, black males are now pulling the trigger on other black males while communities close their eyes as this atrocity plays out. This common occurrence seems to push many victim(s) into isolated groups formulating clouds of insensitivity and a lack of understanding which resides among the innocence throughout the communities.

Issues such as these that are strung up by the noose men will rarely challenge the emotions of black men that are so called "running the streets". After all, it is them that are "in search of" their manhood which leads to the next black man becoming a carrier of the noose and seeking an opportunity to commit a hanging.

Unfortunately, the resolve to what seems to be an acceptable social experience is murder. Too few are mourning these tragic events and too few rarely care. Is this really our culture? Are we really hanging ourselves with a noose and are blind to a spirit of destruction which lurks amongst the black community? If so, why haven't we open our eyes to a new point of view, and if not, who are we to blame if the head (black men), doesn't understand his directions in life?

In the past, it was common to run upon a black male hanging from trees somewhere amongst the sleeping forest. The way black men are killing themselves throughout the communities today, is synonymous to how black men were found hanging from trees during the 1800 and early 1900s. It was also common to see crows feeding off the remains of dead black men while families hoped and prayed for the safe return of their love ones. In a similar fashion, we see the same experience of dying black men because the same outcome is death.

With that being said, instead of finding black men in the corners of river beds, or hanging from a tree, many are now being picked up out of the streets of the same America but the killer is none other than the black man himself.

As mentioned before, it is important to note that the majority of the murders that occurred during the earlier periods of America were carried out primarily by white men. This was common. But even less common were the black men whom were less displaced from their families, and were more bonded and protective of their children and those within the surrounding communities. The only noose to be feared then, was the noose of the system.

Furthermore, the murders of black men in the past by white men were also a methodical experience that was usually pre-planned and carried out with a systematic approach. Now that the KKK and the laws of Jim Crow have relaxed, many unlearned black males are manipulating their own community and the walls are unable to stand because the foundation(of men) has no true substance underneath it.

In other words, violence, drugs and the failure to realize the importance of higher education, all weakens the underlay of this foundation for black males.

Similarly, in the black community the slip knots found on these nooses represents every black male that under minds his community by introducing violence, selling drugs, or committing other acts to destroy black communities. These black men are the new noose men. How so? Because those that are responsible for putting the slip knots in place also share the guilt of lives that become displaced from the family, the community and this world by way of death.

Also, along with this modern day noose is the existence of a limb. The limbs are in place to support these types of hangings. These limbs are the black men looking for a way up, but are suppressing other blacks by moving downward in an effort to make dirty money, and disregard the black community while doing so.

In other words, the noose men of today are familiar with the same neighborhood he is interested in destroying. The purpose for his agenda is created for destruction and nothing else. His biggest enemy is himself, and the next in line are those that look like him. This reason alone allows him (noose men) to choke the life out of his community and other neighboring communities without any conviction for doing so. In other words, he has no love and his demeanor in low places goes undetected by his own people.

These broken limbs (negatively driven male) within the community are dangerous because many have taught themselves that no one cares about them. This method of manipulation makes all of his wrong actions seem right in the eyes of those that are socially suppressed and financially strapped. Once this is accepted by those within the community, then hatred overwhelms the people, and the closure of a finite mind can be worse than death itself, because it creates a slow death.

He also has little respect for the kids and women of the neighborhood, as he searches for ways to not only destroy the black community, but hang these experiences abroad for the world to see. E.g. Certain neighborhoods are so bad, that others that are not from that particular neighborhood can't walk through it. My question is this? How does a young street thug with little education nor insight concerning real estate, take total control over neighborhoods that have strong and viable men living within it? The answer is simple. *When men can't stand and die for what they believe in, then the simple life of "just" living will challenge his presence and weaken his outlook on life.*

Environmentally, this noose man is also good at creating gentrification at the expense of funding his own pockets and decreasing the value on other people's property. Little that he knows, the same money he makes in the streets will ultimately be paid back into the system for his legal woes once he is jailed for hurting those he proclaims to care the most about.

The noose man is also good at establishing crack houses. The fear that he brings upon the community is his weapon. He will easily drive by and shoot up a home, or will kill his so called rival cold blooded in the streets in order to continue his destruction inside the community. It is not the love of money that drives men to do this, but it is their lack of love, respect and consideration from the people he looks the most like and most of all, self hatred for himself.

Within the last five to seven years many of those in the black community have established a street code called "no snitching". No one wants to be a snitch. Even in the face of evil, people have become afraid to stand up for their right, but in an unfortunate twist, some will stand for the wrong and neglect the destruction of their own community. This type of mentality is dangerous and unless men of standard takes a stand to reverse this devastating cause, those who should be heading up the community, will be the reason why communities continue to fall.

Another key element that makes this noose man dangerous is his visibility within the black community. Ironically, it is usually the men that vow to protect the community from other drug dealers, and gang bangers, that somehow are the ones that keep the community suffocating. Because there is no insight into what is really asphyxiating the people, there is an oversight by way of accepting the same men who are hurting the community. This acceptance drains the hope of the people.

Lastly, the only reason we witness this on a continuous scale is secondary to a weakened mindset of many black youths and a distorted view of self identification. What you don't know would not only hurt you, but it can bring a perpetual hurt amongst many generations to come especially if truth and the lack of effort for liberation is not part of the equation.

Releasing the Slip Knot to Stop the Violence

When you fail to acknowledge what you are made of, it is possible to remain blind to everything that stands before you.. Christopher

Anything that holds you captive from releasing your true potentials is dangerous. Anyone that causes you to go against positive beliefs within "you" as an individual will be considered manipulative. Anything or anyone that attaches to you and hold you down in life can be considered a suppressor.

For these reasons, your failures coupled along with your friend's failures, can easily satisfy your emotions, as long as you both are failing. This usually leaves your mind in knots and anytime you find yourself mentally tied up, you risk the chance of becoming asphyxiated aside from achieving positive goals in life.

The formula for releasing the slip knot that causes asphyxiation begins with accountability. Being accountable as a young man gives you the courage to strengthen the inner foundation that morals rest upon and it is the key to unlocking standards within yourself. Without it, it's easy to attract the noose in the streets, because many males are walking around searching to rope a recessive mind young man.

With this attraction, asphyxiation starts when

young men forsake higher education and forego gang banging, drug dealing, and robbing. In the end, not only will you rob others, but you ultimately rob yourself. The reason is simple. The lack of accountability for your actions will cause issues to arise and this leads to character hanging.

On a similar note, when black men are out of place in the home, then the most intricate part of that home is weakened. The weakness rise from what should be the strong links (father) of the home, but their absence is replaced by substituting areas of that home with a liquid underlay. Having a liquid underlay invites the under developed minds of young males to become easily challenged by overriding what little social and moral skills that are already in place, therefore they are constantly in search of.

Consequently, the fight starts with "self". Without an ideal of who you are, nor an understanding of where you desire to go, then you risk the chance of becoming mentally tied up. With this in action, it enables you to effectively enhance your character. Without doubt this exposes you to other characters looking to challenge you for what they feel you should stand for and this in return challenges your boyhood. If this type of fluid underlay continues to exist in black males then the violence we often witness will have no end.

With that being said, these slip knots will continue to entangle hope throughout the black communities and black males will continue to rope each other. The reason stands secondary to the hopelessness and desperation that continues to be the focal point in which many look forward to acknowledging, but without men of standards being in motion there will always be failure.

Lastly, mental growth should being exercised over the experiences of environmental degradation will start with the challenges you put before yourself. **In other words**, start by reading informative books such as the basics of investing, real estate, and self improvement type books. It is ok if you don't like reading because you want be reading for enjoyment. You are now steering your character along a different path way in life. Once you have indulged yourself into this different type of life you will understand that as your intelligence increase, it will not allow you to put yourself into situations that will cause you to choke or asphyxiate your character.

Black Men Dangling

The dysfunctional issues that entangle the lives of many black males are far too grand for anyone to overlook, especially the black man himself. The reason this can't be overlooked is because of the increasing birth rate involving black mothers, and the struggles they are faced with, when black men walk away. *When you father a child, you share life. When you walk out on your child, you damage their life.* When this happens young black males are left dangling.

When black men arise from the streets without character, this experience alone challenges the innocence of their boyhood in an effort to reach manhood. During this challenge anger seems to become the most appropriate way of dealing with issues, and this process inadvertently closes their mind towards self improvement and set up a manrope perimeter.

Having a closed mind causes many to misidentify with self respect and self purpose. From this more focus is hinged upon who should be respecting you and why you deserve to be respected. Too many are growing up wanting respect for character experiences such as, "what hood they are from, or who they are hanging with." This is what I considered to be unlearned. This is where weakness pierces the finite mind, and the number of minds that fall into a similar category reduces strength of character and tightens the slip knot upon droves of black males.

In order to make it right and become a person with true meaning, you must readdress your character. Readdressing your character will entail you putting the focus on elevating your mind, and by doing this, it unties slip knot. If you fail to untie the slip knot, you then dwell in fear of what *you can* achieve and this fear (if it's not dealt with) don't mind pulling the trigger onto someone else's life.

It is possible that this type of fear derives from the inability to feel adequate enough to learn, succeed and walk in such a way in which others will identify you as a young man and not a thug. When these types of strengths are recognized, then black males will begin to walk in their position as young leaders in their communities, and challenge others to walk more positively. This challenge will be to find "self" and recreate their character even within a crucial environment.

While searching and walking in such an experience aside from what you may   have gained much exposure from, it becomes easy to justify the means of selling drugs, being angry and living a life of crime if you never decided to untie yourself. **The reason is simple**. Walking around tied up psychologically is what you have become use to, and anything that feels right, is sometimes considered to be right even if it is wrong in the eyes of him, who will never deny himself.

Apart from the anger sits violence. This violence can easily lead to murdering what they (black men) hate they are protecting themselves against on the outside, but they sorrowfully deal with (by fighting each other) on the inside. When this happens, those bonds that should establish character, emotions and respect, is weakened, making it vulnerable to be roped by the noose.

On the contrary, a real bond within any strong community will always maintain its rigidity and release the strong hold of manropes that may destroy the community. Unlike men that create the slip knots, men of standard have long untied their slip knots by holding themselves accountable and standing for the wrong in order to make it right.

By taking a stance, the bond that real men of standard dwells with, also helps to solidify the positions that men should take and release back into the community to show their concerns, and to annihilate negative issues plaguing the black community. For example, it is no surprise to see young and old black men sitting outside the corner stores or clubs within the inner cities, carrying on about their day to day business. With all due respect to those that may find themselves living like this, they too were once young, but perhaps made choices in which landed them in unfortunate situations. This is where accountability begins, and without its' presence the manipulation of how men should dwell, becomes the downfall that younger black males are being socialized into becoming.

Without black men standing up and initially holding themselves accountable for the continual fall of the black community, the presence of evil will always unveil itself within the streets where the weakest dwells and death can easily prevail. We witness this week after week, and still, black men refuse to Stand!

Without a stance, males involving themselves in robbery and the murdering of others will continue to reap havoc as long as they feel a sense of control over something (community) that is not very well controlled. Without strong men of standards being in control, it ultimately leaves the environment vulnerable to becoming controlled. This is the trap black men have witnessed secondary to weak bonding and it overlaps itself day in and day out.

Through this process of bonding, the source of strength will always be realized because true foundations are formed with knowledge and completed with wisdom. This becomes a necessity only if growth is considered to be the product rising out of a difficult situation. But molding yourself to violence and a life style of being "street" will only interrupts ones' true potentials.

One may ask, how does a bond like this occurs? This type of bonding occurs when we as men invest our time back into our kids and the community. By doing so, it solidifies the strength from the weakest young man and moves upward, birthing strength and rigidness to all young men within a surrounding environment and all that has an ear to hear it.

In order to create such an experience, "time" becomes the investment. This is not a onetime investment, but it is an investment that involves consistency. Without this investment, young thugs will always ruin the communities, and denigrate the social and moral conscious of men and women alike. Furthermore, it is only when your conscious and conviction is overpowered by negative reinforcements, that the ability to see, feel, and recognize wrong, becomes distorted.

Defeating the Noose

In order to defeat the onslaught of the noose that has re- surfaced and is destroying black communities, one must understand the reason behind the noose. The noose is simply there to kill and destroy. This kind of noose will never be defeated as long as (mentally) weak black men continue to satisfy their own desires by using their outer weakness to override what is seen as a token of strengthening, but are lived out in experiences of negative proclivities.

If you are to be a man of strength and valor you must recognize your role involving self and how others will perceive you based on the character you walk in, and the attitude you present. The expression of ignorance through cursing, fighting, and trying to look "hard" is a big sign of weakness although the words are strong.

One of the biggest downfalls of many black men today is their inability to display emotional care towards each other, hence the reason why so many rise up against each other and are victims of race related crimes.

Many black mothers have asked me over and over again, "what can I do to keep my son away from the bad crowd? There are many answers to this question, but one in particular deals with "self awareness." For example, given the way that many youths act, try asking him, are you aware that you can be killed? Are you aware that you don't have money to bail yourself out of trouble if you go to jail, "because I want do it?" And are you aware that your actions in life will determine you outcome? These are basic questions that if overlooked, can lead to many black men hanging themselves. But in reality, in order to defeat anything negative around you, you must recognize that existing "negative" that sometimes commands your presence.

As a teenager, like any other teenager I liked going to clubs and hanging out with the guys. It didn't take me long to realize the danger of getting together with a lot of other black guys. It never failed that someone always started a fight, and the fight usually escalated to somebody going to their trunk to get a gun. This type of stuff happened all the time and it still happens today. I finally realized that I was in control of where I wanted to go, so I stopped going to clubs. Once I opened my mind I realized that being in the presence of guys that were death prone was always an option for me.

This is a prime example of living to die. Unfortunately, it still goes on and many black men are victims of crimes like these all the time. When we see this happening we are witnessing a sense of instability which inadvertently chokes off moral growth. Along with the instability that derive from men committing acts such as these, follows the instability of younger males that are exposed to such tragedy. This is the trickle effect that perpetuates and destroys not only youthful black males, but also settles a damaged lifestyle upon the heads of elementary aged black boys and even younger ones coming up around similar environments.

So, where does one find strength? How does one defeat a noose that has been constricting itself upon young black males for so long? One of the answers go something like this: Strength is not found in being a dealer, gang banging, or robbery. Guys giving their time over to such experiences as these are the type of guys that are searching for a meaning to what they see in the mirror and how to grow that kid in the mirror into a man they have never known.

Initially, I followed that selfish walk along the pathway of life, because I was only concerned about myself. This is another huge problem amongst black males. Instead of us reaching out and creating other positive male figures that are following our footsteps, we engage in groups with each other, and everyone within that small circle lack the ability to positively grow their own character.

When younger black kids don't see strong male figures in their surrounding environment, they usually follow those that are before them. This is the epiphany of a child fighting against a position he has no ideal about, and subsequently he is forced to harden his heart against the negativity of the streets. The end result is forced anger.

Without knowledge, forced anger towards others is simply an instructional tool used for the constriction of this noose.

During the year of 2010 in the city of Augusta, Georgia there were many armed robberies that happened right in the places I am very familiar with. These places are the very places that many of my friends and family members frequent. However, with the ongoing robberies, the fear of being hurt keeps many from trusting areas in which thugs are ruining. Experiences like these keep the symbolic experience of the noose in existence. A large part of the black community is choking itself out of life, and the only ones to blame would be the assailants themselves. So, my question remains. Is it the men or women during these robberies or killings? The answer for the majority is Black Men!

Coupled with knowing the locations of environmental dilapidation, when voices from the communities are never heard and killings go unnoticed or better yet accepted, then the slip knot of this noose has served its' purpose. One should know that nooses serve their purpose when young black men are buried too soon secondary to the violence. Purpose is served when one's inner being is devalued, and their external surroundings are devalued. Purpose is also served when high numbers of black males continually forsake their education, drop out of school, and search for a reason to blame others, because they rather not know the truth, so in return many accept the lie.

All of this relates to a missed alignment of character building which stems from the root of the home, young males actions in school, and the footsteps you take to create your own world.

On one occasion I spoke with a relative about the places he willingly visits, and he told me of the ill fated experiences he's dealt with in his 17 years of life. He spoke of the time that he was robbed, and the time he witnessed his friend being shot and killed. I asked him about some of his favorite places he liked hanging out at, and to no surprise, he liked going to parties. It is never the house party that is bad, but it is what happens at house parties. Especially at parties where large number of young males are in attendance. What usually occur isViolence! *When others don't know their way in life, they have little respect for towards your way of life.*

Although Quincy is an outstanding young man, he failed to realize that hanging in places where violence are prone to happen will soon challenge his character, or even put him at risk of being a murder victim.

One thing to remember is this. If you, as a young man fail to acknowledge "self", and a wayward character continues to put you in places where your heart is not willing to stay, then you are gambling with your life, freedom and respect. The reason is simple: Someone that has less character than you for no reason at all will one day challenge your manhood or challenge the better character they see on the inside of you. In the assailant's mind it doesn't have to be a reason. He (and usually his boys) is driven by what the noose have mentally done. It's just by way of their own ignorance that they look for an opportunity to harm someone else.

For the most part, by defeating the noose found within the black community, not only will you call for an alignment of self, but you will also rise above those negative circumstances that have kept you hostage unto yourself and your community. **In other words**, only you and God know the truth of your heart. If you are walking along a pathway that is misaligned from the truth and you find yourself dwelling in crime, then the oppression of "self", the home, and the community will somehow suffer secondary to what you do wrong, along with what others have decided to do wrong.

Wake up Before It's Prison Time

If you are living your life with negative attachments, then at some point there must be an awakening that occurs. Young black men should never be sent to prison unless they refuse to wake up. Everyone has a conscious and there hasn't been one young man I have mentored that did not understand the consequences for his actions. When one understands the consequences prior going forth with a negative action, then his experiences are only a true product of what his issues are on the inside.

For example, if you are dealing drugs, then you should know that you are on your way to prison. If you are stealing and robbing, then you are on your way to prison. If you are gang banging, then you are on your way to prison. The concept is simple. Whatever it is that you are doing wrong you must wake yourself up, before you find yourself in a prison cell. In other words, *understand you self, and know what you could have in life, before you are **Made** to do, what you have no desire to do.*

Furthermore, without understanding your position in life as a positive and dominant figure, you will always bring wreckage to the forefront of your life.

This misunderstanding may lead to an adverse effect. By watching young black men die in the streets at the hands of other black men, not only does it instill fear, but it instills distrust from one black man to another. When his happens, young black males are taught to protect themselves from other black males and the creation of violence perpetuates because love can't arise.

On a level that have similar experiences, the unfortunate and embarrassing issues that black males subject themselves to by murdering other black males, creates a defensive mode of protection. This mode of protection runs parallel to the pathway of self preservation. In other words, many black males protect themselves from each other by "mean mugging" or killing each other because of misunderstood anger and distrust.

This is where the misalignment of character dwells. You are not born a victim, nor are you born to rob, sell, or go to prison. These are things that you decide to take on when your existence have no meaning. Part of your existence involves nurturing, teaching, extending love and life to those, in which you have the privilege of coming in contact with, so why not live.

In the end, the argument is useless when it comes down to the truth of who murders who, and why the murders took place. The sad part is this: When you see young black males going in this direction, it is all secondary to them being asleep, as those worthwhile achievements sit in front of them. Their inability to wake up, will ultimately confines them unto a place in which they are then controlled.

Blaming someone else for your violent activities only

helps to camouflage your wrong doings, as you walk backwards in the shadows of what you always known to be wrong, and the convictions many ignore while being confronted with the right.

To prevent this type of failure and loosen the noose, it must begin with how your mind is utilized. If you utilize your mind to involve yourself in negativity, then you casually create a slip knot of the noose that will eventually affect somebody's life along with your own. **In other words**, you are still sleeping through all of your negative actions, and if you refuse to wake up, then your consequences will be your wake up call. When experiences like these happen, it occurs not only because of a weak mindset you have given yourself over to, but entraining negativity soon challenges your weakness, and ties up your future.

A weak mind will tell you to drop out of school because education is not working for you. A weak mind will tell you to involve yourself in a gang and hurt others that are not wearing the same colors or are not from the same neighborhood. A weak mind will have you carry a gun around looking for an occasion to rob someone or protect yourself from someone else, all because you are hanging in the wrong area. A weak mind will also tell you to smoke, sell, and do anything negative that will bring temporary satisfaction, but in the end, your consequences will be long term.

On the other hand, having a sound mind and the right attitude is what will propel you along the right pathway of life. In all essence, when the right character is in place, the likelihood of males within bad communities will escape asphyxiation from the hands of other men who may also lack purpose and character, but in order to liberate, youths must be willing to educate.

Standing alongside of this is the invitation for bonding which invites a sense of closeness, and solidification. Apart from the bonding which is definitely needed between positive black males and weaker black males, if one is not able to loosen the slip knot that is suffocating the black community, then it will continue to distort growth and character seen amongst the weaker black men. Hence the reason why so many follow simple fads.

In the end, before purpose and character can be dressed up within you as the individual, it will always take acknowledgement and accountability to pry open the mind. There must be an open mind to see the problem of black males if change will ever take place. This failed continuation of not recognizing the total covering of good character will also continue to present itself and purpose will never find its' way outside the hole of the slip knot. Therefore, waking up in a prison cell will be the case, and black male imprisonment will only benefit the system at the expense of those black males that are unwilling to learn.

Death of a Young Black Male and Female

During the month of January 2010 in the city of Augusta, Ga. a young black man was shot and killed. Brandon Taylor responded to a knock on the window on this particular night and was shot. Two black males were arrested and charged with his murder. These two assailants apparently tried to get revenge from supposedly being shot at while walking through the neighborhood. The outcome is a senseless death, many years in prison, and hurting family members that suffer the loss on both sides.

During the month of February 2010 in the city of Augusta, Ga., a young 16 year old black female was shot to death by a young black male. Tykiah Palmer was shot once in the chest. She died after slapping this young man. Not only did Tykiah meet such a senseless and untimely death, but she was expecting her first baby. Shortly after Tykiah arrived at the MCG emergency room, she underwent an emergency caesarian, according to WAGT 26. Unfortunately, the baby also died a short time after being born. The assailant was a 15 year old black male name Loviet N. Edwards. He was charged with two counts of murder at the age of 15 years old.

Hanging Limbs in the Black Community

When one thinks of the black community and the many issues plaguing the black community, the term "hood" comes to mind. What we refer to as the "hood" is considered the "hood" because of its reference to crime and violence, and not a place of comfort. In general, a hood is anything that covers or protects the head part of an individual or substance that appears uncovered.. Without a covering, there is little protection, and when those whom are the protectors remove themselves from the keepsake of their community, then, boys within the hood confront these experiences and struggle against a mindset called "ghettoism."

Usually, the hood is not considered a peaceful place to dwell, but it is perceived as a lowly place hosting bad experiences. Those black males that rave about the hood, are the same ones that are instrumental in the negative activities that goes on in the hood. The bad experiences that are created and redistributed back into an environment already suffering, is not only carried out by black males, but the same black males becomes anti- cops when having police protection is more than necessary.

So, how does an environment grow if the men within that environment retards its' growth? If it is perceived that most buildings will surely collapse provided that it has a weak foundation, then, how does black men seen in crime ridden environments considered themselves to be strong men?

The truth is, they are really the weakest vessels looking to control that which is uncontrollable. The willingness to influence negative actions is what retards the growth of the community.

I have watched and heard countless young brothers refer to their dwelling place as the "hood." *When one is unlearned or don't have the desire to learn, they retard themselves away from their own potentials.* This type of retardation is then coupled with others that may have a kindred spirit and the behavior that can be embraced invites a lifestyle that is uncanny but at the same time equally yoked.Having come from a very dilapidated environment myself, I've even thrown words around loosely when I was younger. However, unknown to a finite mind, words like "my hood, my nigga, and other slang words we easily embrace for the sake of coolness, often starves the mind of the ability to think effectively about detrimental issues, and in return minimize self worth because nothing in close proximity feels like an asset.

Onward, when we refer to our neighborhoods as the hood, we unknowingly speak self and environmental demise in a way that seems acceptable, but at the same time it is a verbal noose that dangles from a limb of life. This is another way people embrace destruction.

It becomes easy to accept once you have entrained negativity and establish an emotional attachment to it. The attachment becomes a part of you because after a while, "that's all you know!" By doing this, it causes one to be conditioned more by their surroundings, and inadvertently suppress the ability to overcome those experiences that seems natural.

When this happens, there is an artificial empowerment of the weaker mind to become a part of something that is failing. Having said that, when black males fail to realize the risk that comes with the fall, it then prevents them from rising above the circumstances which confronts them. Furthermore, *it seems only right to fight against another man which have similar experiences, rather than defeat the circumstances which rarely goes away.*

Aside from the aforementioned, the only thing that will come together out of experiences like these are the tightening of the loop holes found dangling at the end of the "noose." Without doubt, when the noose hole is tightened, there is a choking effect. It occurs each time black men result to violence or sell of drugs within the same area they claim to love and live within. This is known as manipulation by way of embracing destruction, and over time, black males become the limb in which the noose is tied around making Jim Crow seem right against everything blacks fought against.

When one considers the enlightening of "self" and step out of the trap that proves to be negative, then self improvement becomes that missing link. This will only occur when you deny those negative actions the right to take growth and dwell within you. For me, this type of growth started when I took the time to think! Now, that I have open my eyes to a microscopic part of wisdom in which God has granted me I realize that I am a part of this world, and not a destructive seed within this world, and I'm still a young black man.

Other issues that will prevent you from hanging yourself is the fact that you are aware of how to untie your mind with all the negativity you have been taught. If the mind, which is a power source, grows without being informed or trained, it then becomes easy to justify your wrong actions, because you have lived without understanding. From this, it becomes easy to embrace manipulation by beckoning one to stay true to the hood, when in fact, it is the criminals themselves who are usually the ones affecting the hood while proclaiming to be true.

You must remember this. Anything that affects you garners the rights to attach itself to you. Being comfortable with things that have negative attachments, lie along the same lines as having an emotional attachment. When you are affected by negative experiences and find comfort with it, a part of you is challenged just as your emotions are challenged making it an easy way to die.

On a different front, some black men rather stay true to the hood because the hood has allowed them to have the manpower they otherwise would not have in other places outside of the hood. It is not that black men can't have that power outside of the hood, but it becomes the struggle against "self" and their ability to demonstrate self belief. In other words, those black men that are destroying the hood, perceive this place as a battlefield in which they try to control. Their weakness lies within their inability to challenge themselves to more positive experiences out of fear of failure, therefore they hang each other.

This is why it is easy to become comfortable in knowing how to control the streets they are doing wrong on. But unknowingly, no one ever wins. The only outcome is prison or the grave yard. No one will ever win the battles upon the grounds they are fighting upon, because the real battle is of the mind. The ultimate battlefield or plantation becomes the prison yards.

If you are involved or are seeking to be involved in drugs, robbery, stealing, gang banging etc., without the knowledge of understanding yourself first, then it is possible you are seeking power to control something or someone that is weak. This weakness will always lead you to confront the real enemy in your life at some point and time. And the real enemy is "you." The type of weakness that many black males run into gives them the ideal that they are strong, but in reality their weakness will only carry the ideal that they are hard core men, when in reality, they are full of weakness. Therefore, all of these experiences in a nutshell explode into shooting or stabbings that takes another's life.

With that being said, in order to understand yourself, you must critique yourself. The power and respect you may be seeking in these experiences is what will ultimately destroy you. It is said that more than majority of black men that are in the jails or the prisons are their secondary to what they did unto another black man, or their black community. In other words, they hung themselves from the branches within their own surroundings or they harmed those they are the most familiar with in their life, other black men.

In the end, this power is not an effective power, but it's a defective power. Without doubt, this kind of power that is demonstrated in such a contained but gentrified area of the mind can never be seen as exploring the experiences of integrity, but it's a diluted power that survives by way of negative activity.

Refusing to Be Hung

At the other end of the spectrum, if you are thinking, or living this way, then you will have no choice but to become this way. My reason for saying this starts with the shameful truth that is seen in today's society. Throughout many inner city communities, too many black men have either displaced themselves from the family, by going to prisons (mainly for what they do unto other black men), being hooked on drugs, or just plain inactive in places where they should be proactive.

Real men living within a community and trying all they can to embrace positive experiences with other young brothers is an exception, only if there is consistency in improving other young lives. But if you are defective, meaning: (always just chilling, no job, or seeking for ways to deceive someone) then you become part of the infection within the community and environments like these will rarely heal.

On the other hand, if you are infectious to your surroundings, the breakdown of that community becomes less probable to heal as long as you maintain that infection. This healing will not take place secondary to what many black men are aiming for (drugs, etc.). This leaves a wound on the community that is less likely to heal because the strength (black men) will rarely acknowledges its' weakness.. Situations like these leave boys hanging out in the streets, which is known as "boys in the hood". This phrase is easily coined because it is difficult for boys to override mental impoverishment, when men of standard are not in their respectful places.

From a spiritual standpoint, the Bible says, "bound up in the heart of a child is foolishness." When one acts out foolishly it empowers the "noose" and by empowering the noose, it stagnates the ability for a young and vibrate mind to open up and perform anything effectively.

In respect to any environment worth living in, it is never the place itself that is bad. It is usually the men within the environment who have denied themselves the truth, and their way of understanding life involves choking out the truth to bring forth the wrong. All of this occurs when men don't understand leadership and "hanging" becomes a way of life.

Furthermore, the manipulation that many black men embrace by proclaiming to be men also challenges their mind from operating at its complete capacity, when in truth, they are grownups doing child like things. One can easily wrap their mind around such a dilapidated experience and remain there for years. This occurs because the focus becomes geared towards competing at the street level, instead of a level considered to be a higher and more positive level. This higher level involves moving ahead in the world (primarily through higher education) and understanding the importance of what has been given to you, and how to make the best of those resources.

In order to move away from violence, robbing or dealing, you must become aware of your destiny. Without this awareness you will never allow your mind to compete for anything good, but continually subject yourself to everything bad. How so? Because people surrounding you, may possibly be carrying similar desires on the inside. Two or more bad spirits can never birth anything positive. This can create the sense of competing against the nonsense that surrounds you, rather than elevating yourself to higher levels of achievements and compete against things that matter rather than things that keep you from moving upward in life.

Senseless Death of Young Men

During the month of May 2010, Tollie Mitchell was shot and killed while in his car. It was later discovered that the two accomplices were friends of the Mitchell family. These guys robbed and killed Tollie while meeting for a drug deal. Tollie was shot in the neck. He died and left behind two kids.

During the month of September 2010, a 19 year old was shot at a gas station in Atlanta, Georgia with a AK-47. La Derrick was sitting in his car at the gas station along with his pregnant girlfriend and his 8 month old baby in the back seat. As seen on the store camera, two assailants exited their car in broad day light with others standing around, and one approached La Derrick's car. Moments later the shooter open fire into the car without any regards to who was in the car. La Derrick drove off, but later died trying to get help. His pregnant girlfriend was also shot sending her into a premature labor. The baby in the back seat was not hit.

During the month of May 2009 in Augusta, Ga. a 20 year old Tremayne Cobb was shot in the head and pronounced dead at the scene of the crime. Two young black males were responsible for the shooting.

This ongoing battle in the black community is not something that the world cares to witness, if the "black man" himself does not care to recognize it. In the past, the Afro-American community was seen as some of the most unified people in America. But over a period of time, black men, whom are supposed to be the leaders in the black community started neglecting their duties and gravitated towards selfish desires within gentrified places. This left younger black males without a sense of direction. With that being said, anyone without a sense of direction will also suffer from the lack of shared love and positive male nurturing.

In addition, without the understanding of peace and love, the pathway of one's mind becomes more susceptible to reaping havoc. Not only is this being seen in the streets of too many black communities, but the forerunner for which is partly responsible for how minds are shaped and conformed trickles down through negative music, onto the ears of unequipped minds. Unequipped minds allow this settlement because they are unaware of this "dangling noose" constructed by black males.

But overall, the problem stemming from the black community being left to fend for itself is all secondary to how black men have displaced themselves and nothing more. Furthermore, if unequipped black males continually move forward without the understanding of positive social and moral skills, then we will continue to see a disconnection from male to male, from generation to generation. This disconnection will lead to a continual decline of social morals and will never display a continual flow of togetherness secondary to the negative impact of inconsistency, placated onto the minds of unequipped black males. Without this social improvement, the only type of consistency we will continue to witness is the consistency of violence.

Who are we blaming?

The embarrassment of the black crime we witness leaves many of us in denial as we quickly downplay how serious it really is. This downplaying of what young black men are doing to each other causes many of us to search for someone or something to put the blame upon. The truth is, is there anyone else to blame other than ourselves?

When I travel throughout different neighborhoods and witness young men walking around wearing the same gang colors, I instantly think, where are the fathers that care? If dad is dead or in prison, then where are the uncles, grandfathers or any strong male presence. This is the beginning of how young men get hung.

All the while, we as black people make the most noise when it comes to our civil rights, but we deny ourselves the truth about this murderous situation going on with black males throughout America and quickly push this under the rug.

Black men shouldn't simply make proactive noises when issues are brought up against us as a culture of people when we ourselves stand along the side lines witnessing the mass murders of our own black males. Moreover, too many of our black males are not being held accountable for the crimes they do within their own communities. Not only are many black males not holding themselves accountable for their own issues at hand, but too many black females enable black men from becoming that in which they are capable of becoming. This perpetuates the situation and their accountability for anything is even more minimized when women enable young males.

I must add, the issues involving blacks being wrongfully beaten or killed by cops are wrong, but even more wrong is the continuation of black crime that no one has paused and too many have learned to embrace. In other words, too many are willing to hang themselves, because they don't understand themselves.

During the month of November in Waynesboro, Georgia, 14 years old John Preston was shot and killed by another young black man. I was able to attend the funeral of such a senseless killing. I must say that this was the saddest day of 2010. This young man had great ambitions and was simply trying to bring peace to a disturbance that was taking place amongst other young black men. A fourteen year old kid being killed! That is crazy. Not only was he killed, but the father of this same fourteen year old was killed in the same county during the month of January 2011. In other words: Less than two months after losing his son to violence, the father of John Preston is killed himself.

Tragic cases like these will never stop until stronger black men take a stand. Taking a stand in cases like this one should have called for the black men in this county moving towards peaceful means by utilizing meetings to prevent further issues like this one from happening. Even after the killing of this father at this particular night club, the strong men within that community should have been taking a stand to remove this club since it isn't the first time men have been killed at this place. This is what being proactive entails.

A Dilapidated Mindset

The black crime that is witnessed throughout the cities within the U.S. brings to the forefront a need for truth concerning black men, and a way to re-strengthen the weak and unlearned mind. Without a re-assessment of these issues at hand, the young and wayward minds of black youths will continue to falter, and this will perpetuate down through the lineage of males stunting the growth of their seeds that follows.

When the minds of young black men become dilapidated, their thinking becomes distorted in how they perceive each other. Some are perceive as enemies right off the back, secondary to where they are from, or what school they attended. This is more than ridiculous. Some are perceived as trying to be "gangsta" and this sends off a message of disrespect that is hard to be overlooked by a weak mind because a weak mind desires to be noticed.

Continued experiences like these can easily implode, sending out pieces of mistrust, anger, and violence right into the pathway of other young black males looking to increase the friction. This implosion of anger, or "I'll get with you" type of attitude always causes blindness to the truth that is living right among them, but rarely causes one to open their eyes to factual ignorance. For many, when this occurs, a wall of anger is constructed and reasoning is of no use. Not because of what is before them, but because what many refuse to address as a self related issue.

At times it may take years to penetrate walls of anger. However, during this process, dilapidation has its due process and finite minds can never impute strength into the mind of others that have kindred like spirits.

Alongside the process of mental dilapidation comes the inability to understand an increase elevation of the mind. You can be or act anyway you desire, but you must not forget the things you expose yourself unto. The reason is this: Dilapidation is that experience that starts within the mind, and protrudes outward and it can only take place when something is ignored and the responsibility of failure to acknowledge it falls short of what it should be. Having said that, too many male children are ignored! With this happening, the mental experience of dilapidation will deal with the break down or decay of something that once had good standing but is now decaying secondary to a weak foundation.

This weak foundation that is found in the lives of many black males, are the missing fathers, and the unwilling participation of black males in the community that are willing, to do something consistently positive. It works both ways. Just as young black men run around trying to be dealers, gangsta, or thugs on the streets, they can easily change and influence younger black males by assisting with education, or become a neighborhood teacher to younger black males that are dying for male attention.

Aside from fathers being displaced from their kids, there is also a lack of male love and bonding. Not only have I seen this in the lives of too many young males, but I have experienced it myself. I now understand that when I have love and respect towards people, it can never rob, kill, steal or disrespect others because the foundation of respect is created on the inside.

After experiencing such a lack of necessities, I also realize that anything that starts to break down must have, at some point in time, been in good standing. By withholding such necessities as love, encouragement, and quality time, it ultimately makes it more difficult for any male to test the waters of confidence and express true measures towards surrounding men.

On the contrary, some young men build confidence by way of trying to prove how "hard" one is against another. The only difference is this. This testing method minimizes the shield of shared love and black males become the target of violence at a young age, because by nature we constantly look for something to validate our self worth and our self value.

For example, one must wonder why certain neighborhoods or streets are bad to go into. The neighborhoods are not bad simply because it is impoverished. It is usually bad, because black men have decided to control a territorial space. This happens because they lack the ability to control their own inner ambitions, and search outwardly to control that which can't be controlled. Therefore, if you neglect yourself from being educated, gaining knowledge, and entraining wisdom, you are simply living to no avail, and the likelihood of mental decay is possible.

Moreover, it is not easy to detect the issues at hand especially when you give yourself over to thinking that a negative lifestyle is the only way out. Over a period of time, this process of dilapidation will find its way into the crevices of a weak foundation (mind) and it goes something like this. The father was not involved in the young man's life. Dilapidation! There was a lack of true male love and bonding. Dilapidation! No spiritual foundation to support good morals and character. Dilapidation! All of these are examples of a dilapidated mind.

If you never wake up to understand yourself, you will never truly know yourself! The reason is obvious. You will never know your true potentials because you would have never challenged yourself to do things positive rather than doing things negative.

Usually, situations like these are passed on to our children, and our children's children without hesitation. From this, when men fall from their position in life, it's easy for the surroundings to fall victim to a similar process. Overall, men standing up to teach other young men is the kind of strength that black males must display if change is to come.

Without taking this stance, young men that are unmade will never recognize any value within themselves because at 14 or 15 years of age, your thinking capacity is limited and foolish actions usually obstructs your way. Therefore, when older men, who are stronger vessels, make crucial mistakes by walking away, they are able to quickly pass on these negative experiences which are entrained by unlearned minds and carried out by various means.

Unfortunately, when a young black man finds himself in situations like these he will never realize that his own self neglect will only hinder and denigrate the most important asset he has in his life. That is "himself." If you never wake up to understand yourself, then you will never truly know yourself. You will never realize your true potentials because you will have never challenged yourself to anything positive beyond the position you stand upon. The reason can be found in how accustomed you may have been around the things that were negative. All of these devices are what encompasses the noose within the black community.

It also depicts the weakness discovered upon the unwillingness to learn and where there is an unwillingness to learn, there's never a reason to succeed.

The Power of a Noose

What is it that sets a strong and influential young man apart from the negative influences of other young men? The answer is, his ability to walk in a leadership role and the denying of negative actions his friends try and impose upon him. The one thing that many young men on the streets do not understand is the power they carry within themselves to either influence in a good way, or the damage they create in a bad way. The type of power I am speaking of is not the power to carry a gun or the power to run drugs, but the power to influence others in a positive way. Everyone have a source of power. Now, whether you use this power for knowledge or trickery it is all up to you. But in the end, consequences will never be hindered from impacting the very ones that invited them.

When young black men misuse their minds and abilities to negate from what is right, then this symbolic noose has its' way of expressing its' power by tightening up the slip knot. The unfortunate part is that, the very people that are misled are the same people who are proactive when cops and other intruders hurt black men within the same community, that many (dealers, etc) themselves are destroying. This is an example of what it depicts:

As long as black youths kill each other in the streets,

it's really not that bad. Blacks must ensure that no one else come into our community and kill our young boys. Otherwise, we will march!!

This is a distorted view and it twist the truth into becoming a falsified lifestyle. Falsifying such experiences will continual to accept the crimes perpetuated by many black males especially when the truth is continued to be shield by the enemy who lives within the same community and walks along with the black man.

Besides, this is weak behavior carried out by those who hurt the black community the most. Not only is this weak behavior, but it can be seen as reactive behavior rather than proactive behavior. If you hold a firecracker in your hand, it is usually harmless to you, as long as it is not ignited. It is obvious that firecrackers have the potentials to do damage, but if it is never lit, the damage can never be done.

On the other hand, when it is lit, it becomes reactive. It now has the power to do damage. This can be seen as reactivity. There are too many people within the black community that are willing to fight when it's time to fight against the system, but often times, give up the fight when it is our own that is carrying the noose and hanging thousands of black men on a yearly basis.

When one is proactive, it does not take someone placing a fire under you in order to get you started. When you are proactive, you have the will and the power to stand when you hear of young males being shot in the streets. Pro-activity will also cause you to reach, teach, and inform young people based on life experiences you may have endured. It should never take an act from the system being

unjustified, in order to push the black community towards reactivity. The black community should already be proactive!

During the month of October in Augusta, Georgia 2010 a young black man at the age of 16 was shot in the back of the head while driving. This young man ended up wrecking his vehicle secondary to the gunshot wound he sustained. The next day the news covered the story, but no one else gave much press on it. This kid was 16 years old!! There was no public outcry, considering it was the 30th or 31st murder in Augusta. There was no push to bring the killer to justice. There was nothing. This is how the noose maintains its' power. Even the black churches within the same community refused to stand outside their walls, and take back what too many black males have already taken from the people. That would be the sense of trust and hope.

Without implementing hope and trust, negativity becomes the imposing factor. Negative power is always dangerous because it settles upon the pathway of those who care the least. With the acts of self hatred, violence, and murder, this cycle of experiences will not cease. Why is this? The reasons can be secondary to many of the young men that abandon their morals. Many are willing to abandon them because the standards of being a real man may cause one to acknowledge himself and too many young black males turn away from this acknowledgement and act as if it does not exist.

I have watched and heard countless young brothers refer to their dwelling places as the "hood." Having come from a very dilapidated environment myself, I've even thrown the word around loosely. Phrases like "my hood, my nigga, and other words we sometimes embrace starve our minds of the ability to think effectively, and minimize our own standards without giving it a second thought. This is another formula of the noose. Before long it becomes a way of life and we somehow continue to make it cultural. From a cultural standpoint it sears into our attitude and is displayed throughout one's character and in our conversation.

When you refer to your environment as the hood you unknowingly speak self and environmental demise without true knowledge of what is being said. By the use of your own tongue, speaking in such a way empowers the weak to be a part of something that is already failing, while overlooking the escape route to higher knowledge. This is self detainment and in the end, the only thing that seems to come together is the tightening of the loop hole found dangling at the end of the "noose."

For this reason, I now realize that the hood or a dilapidated environment, deals more with an unlearned mind, rather than the environment itself. This is a place where one will not only acknowledge that hardship occurs, but a place one has created mentally in their mind leading many black males into living out what they fight against, and struggle to have any respect for.

Moreover, unlike the Jews during the 1930's whom were forced into ghetto camps by the Nazis, many blacks gladly embrace such a term and such a place as a mindset, that it carries a denigrating spiritual heaviness upon their lives and have perpetually robbed many African Americans of a truth that is rarely taught.

If the mind, which is a power source, is untrained, it then becomes easy to embrace such term like, my hood, my nigga, or phrases like, "I'm so ghetto." The fight against such atrocities like these disconnects many Afro- Americans from competing in a wholesome way. While growing up in the hood, I could never see the whole wide world because I was blinded by my own world which was the hood. Little did I know, my world wasn't interested in teaching me how to become educated, how to become financially savvy, nor how to increase by way of obtaining self knowledge. Most of the things I learned were things that were designed to set me back, rather than place me forward. And by the way, other black males were my teachers.

Onward, many black men rather stay true to the hood because the hood allows them to have the man power they would otherwise not have in other places outside of the hood. If you are involved or are seeking to be involved in drugs, robbery, stealing, gang banging etc., then remember this. *Without the knowledge of understanding "yourself", it becomes easy to find yourself in search of something powerful, when in fact, it will render you powerless. The bad thing is this*: As a young man, the power and respect you are seeking to extract from bad experiences, is what will destroy you.

On a different note, young brothers on the streets compete for power and they seek this negative power without considering the type of asphyxiation it brings upon themselves and their community. Nevertheless, the power they are seeking is not the power that will propel them in the right direction, but it is the power that will arrest their own conscious, spirit, and physical being in due time.

In all essence, this type of power is not an effective power, but it is a defective power. This defective power that derives from how the noose is created and the people that are hung by it has been the bait that many black men have taken time after time and in doing so, many families have suffered tremendous loss.

In addition, the kind of power that is demonstrated in gentrified areas of the mind is not a power of integrity, but some utilize it as a power to fulfill their own statue by way of wanting to control the elements they can never control. I am simply referring to the constriction of the noose, and the hanging of black males. This always end up in crime, because they head is really underneath.

At the other end of the spectrum, if you are living

this way, this kind of thinking will surely camouflage the truth of what the ideal of being a man is all about and have you thinking that you're straight "hood" when it's really straight ignorance.

Without doubt, the time spent trying to be "street" and thuggish, will always rob you of the time you could be using to educate yourself to a higher level, accomplish positive goals, or build good character. In the end, if you rob yourself of your own growth and dwell in ignorance, then when you are sent to jail or prison, the time spent in this incarcerated camp is only served out by you and YOU only.

The Becoming of Positive Men

How does a young man become something he has never been shown how to become? How do young men become men of standards if their minds aren't opened for change? How does one substantiate a need or want if they are part of the problem? And how does a man walk away from a seed he willingly plants, but have no desire to see grow?

When knowledge is undeveloped in a young man's mind the foundation of his character is unstable. Before character can be produced one must first stand along the sidelines of life, and witness the mannerisms of becoming what can easily be destroyed. I'm speaking of your LIFE!

One of the simplest experiences in becoming a young man is the understanding of who you are in life, before others have the chance to figure you out. Many young men have not only died senseless deaths but are wasting their time away in prisons throughout the United States because they fail to pull a positive character to the forefront of their senses.

When you fail to recognize the substance within yourself, you will either influence someone towards a negative outcome, all because you fail to stand up for the righteousness within yourself. When you as a young man are seeking to change and gain responsibility, then by dressing yourself up with standards starts in the confinement of you as the individual. Even as early as third grade or lower, young men should be learning how to set their alarm clocks for school in the morning. This is a start of responsibility. Not only should you set your alarm clock, but getting your clothes ready the night before adds to being responsible for your own actions. If you forget to do this, start all over again, until you begin to understand the importance of meeting the goals that you set as a young man. This is where the beginning of setting standards and growing your character begins.

School is another place where you as a young man should be willing to prove yourself. School is your job, and in a sense, it is symbolic of the world hosting lots of kids that are on a learning ground. If you are a troublemaker in school, most likely, the same will happen once you graduate, or drop out of school. If you are hanging with the dealers, the bangers, and other crowds that are going   nowhere, then the only place you will end up will be the jail or the grave yard. Statistics has shown this over and over again.

According to the Schott State's report of Black males and education, black youths in Georgia alone is under the 50% graduation rate. Some states such as New York city during the year of 2007/2008 had rates that were in the mid 20% range for graduation. The importance of higher education will undoubtedly elevate your mind and liberate you from ignorance. But without higher education the chances of challenging yourself and moving upward in society becomes an experiment that can sometimes be lonely.

To put it differently, young boys fall through the cracks on the streets in constant search of their manhood when they do not know their way. In many cases, while in search of their identity as young men they become vulnerable to the devices that appear to be good, but these devices have devastating consequences. These devices include selling drugs, smoking weed, arm robbery, stealing, etc. Before long, the same young men that are out in the streets start to aimlessly compete for a room in the jail or prison system.

One particular case in point happened during the month of May 2011. Four young black men took it upon themselves to rob and kill an 81 year old man that was known to use oxygen just to get around with on a daily basis. This was a tragic event. It was an event that could have been stopped, however, ignorance stood in the way of each of these young boys, and prevented wisdom from surfacing.

Not only did this 81 year old man die a tragic death, but these teenagers killed him as he sat in the comfort of his home bothering no one. Out of the four young men that were involved in this crime, no one had the boldness to tell the other to call off the robbery. Ignorance seemingly overshadowed their finite minds to the point of them thinking that they could elude capture after murdering this innocent man in the comfort of his home. Luckily, all were captured and the youngest being at the age of 15 years old, along with the others will spend the rest of their life serving out a robbery, and murder conviction.

When men fail to realize what they stand for, the probability of failure becomes more apparent. When negative experiences are not learned and one has no desire to change, then "death" becomes the ultimate experience that implements change away from this world.. In other words, you must choose, because change MUST occur.

Consequently, when we hear or witness kids being killed or are killing in the streets, there is an unheard cry out for help that resonates throughout the world. Unfortunately, the world may be too far away to recognize one small cry, and communities remain too deaf to embrace the pain that our youths endure.

On the other hand, it only takes one strong mind man to overturn one weak mind kid. This is how change occurs. But when the strength of a man's mind is replaced with the vulnerability of choosing a life of drugs, or crime, then the resulting experience is incarceration. Mental incarceration!

To say the least, when one is incarcerated, it usually brings all things back to remembrance of how one should conduct themselves and this lesson is recognized once they are in prison, which is a bit too late.

More so than that, once the release from prison occurs, the struggle to commit to maintaining a changed mind is usually the battle if you remain blind to the renewing of your character. This remains to be an ongoing battle because too many young men wrestle with the principalities of an environment that has no mind to change rather than wrestle with "self", an entity that does have a mind to change.

Only man himself have the ability to change his own mind, but before this occurs, your mind has to be readjusted for change, in order for conformity to be recognized.

Again, change starts with a desire to conform the mind and the recognition of a need to change. If one doesn't recognize that he is a part of an equation that either involves selling, gang banging, robbing, or killing, then change will never occur because there is no self denial. Sometimes when you are looking for change, it becomes difficult to deny yourself of the bad things you do. The reason it becomes difficult is secondary to the feeling you extract such negative experiences. In other words, you find the reason to justify all the bad things you do, but look outwards to blame others for the consequences you have to face.

On a different level, mental strength is created from the good things you do in life, and not the bad things. The mental strength of men should always supply (with knowledge), each and every vessel that is attached to that man, if he is to consider himself a leader. These vessels can easily run throughout the confinements of home, communities, churches, schools, and social clubs. These vessels include male youths, mentees, or some child you may not know personally, but they find themselves in the vicinity of your presence and you now have the chance to influence them positively.

As a real man with true leadership and potentials, your presence alone has the power to liberate weaker minds that are entangled if you find yourselves worthy of being a leader. Onward, the continued lacking of black male standards and character will always keep younger black men in search of a purposeful good.

Black men must first acknowledge it before they can demonstrate it. Without acknowledgment, it is easy to become an infection in the community and all infections are susceptible to spreading outward bringing about a severe epidemic of crime. An untrained mind is a baking ground for crime and self denigration. It is a baking ground because many are left with trying to understand how to be, where to go, and how to grow.

With that being said, the one thing that make infections (thugs, etc.) bad within a community, is its' ability to spread over other finite minds throughout the same community. Unfortunately, many of the finite minds are the males running around selling the drugs in order to make the cash, and making the stash in order to be sent to jail.

When young men carry such a resistant strand of infection like this, it can become difficult to heal the wounds of the community because the vessels within that community are lacking a vast supply of male mentoring, male bonding, and higher male standards.

By the same token, God gave man the ability to shape, form, structure and strengthen both girls and boys. However, if there is no challenging of "self" to impute proper knowledge into those that are surrounded by man "himself", then **failure** becomes the result of his own inconsistencies, and his misused abilities.

Stringing the Noose

When fathers go to jail for any period of time, they usually leave behind their children, their mommas, and their baby's momma. My question is, whose the man now? The evidence of this seen time and time again amongst black males signifies the stringing of the noose. Not only is the noose made to be widened during this stage of their life, but the process of stringing it alone all falls upon the black man in the black community.

Most men have a strong desire to not only be respected, but if they are fathers, they should have a desire to lead their children (especially boys). But the conflict begins when children have to suffer secondary to negligence of fathers who should be demonstrating power and love, but instead misunderstood their destiny and are now making their kids suffer.

Because negligence is felt and seen early on amongst black males, it is also common to see the construction of anger, and the fear black males endure secondary to the security some may never grab hold of in their lifetime.

As a young child, my father left me at the age of 9 years old. Not only was I angry about the times that he was not around in my life, but that anger translated into violence or some other devious act, inflicted upon the environment I was raised up in. This is how nooses within the black communities are strung. The unfortunate part dwells among the young minds left to suffer secondary to the lack of direction by stronger men, or the lack of understanding good character.

This pain usually falls onto the family that is left behind.. This pain weighs on the family both emotionally and financially. The pain of trying to raise money to go his (imprisoned dad) bond. The high expense imposed onto families to talk to fathers from prison when they make collect calls from a prison cell. The pain of having to drive the distance to see fathers in prison. And the pain of explaining to a young girl or boy that their father is in prison because of his own selfish desires.

As a man, it is your duty to provide, but if those provisions are not there, causing one to create negativity against yourself, your family, and your community then it still want be available if you decide to sell drugs, and be sent to prison once you are caught. This is emotional pain, and no matter how you try to right the wrong, kids are scarred behind this emotionally, and they seek to find answers by any means necessary. This is another way of stringing the noose. After all, those young boys in the streets without strong fathers or mentors, will usually kill what they emotionally long for, but easily rise up against the shadow's of a neighbor.

All of these become stressors over time while trying to maintain communications with a father who decided to forsake everything underneath him. And by the way, attorney fees and probation fees were never mentioned, but they can be incredible fees that impose financial damage on everyone.

Thereupon, when a noose exist, its primary purpose is to be adjusted until there is a point of collapse. Nooses are pulled onto the community and the slip knot collapses death is imminent. When we see the dealers on the corner, the pimps on the streets, and the gang bangers, we are witnessing the tightening of a noose upon the people within the community. This loitering of young men in this respect leads to atrophy. It happens because men are not being used purposefully within the neighborhoods.

Instead, there is more of an invitation geared towards negativity and such experiences like these settle upon the shoulders of men within the community and births a trickle like effect. This type of effect trickles downward until the pulse of life is weakened within that community. Having anything that is weak will usually lack the strength to grow succumbing to detrimental experiences that are overwhelming.

After experiencing situations such as these, it becomes easy to point the finger at the existing situation, and look towards a stronger entity to right the wrong. For example, many people blame the government, policemen, politicians, teachers, and everyone else except "self" for the failures and high incarceration of black men. Failure to recognize ones' own inadequacies is usually dealt with by pushing the blame in a different direction. The visibility of a disruptive community is strongly to blame on the failure of men and their inability to become what they fail to stand up for, is consequently felt by others.

Overall, sometimes we as a people look for a reason to dislike the present memories of what the past once held our ancestors hostage to. But perhaps this is why it takes a lot to mobilize a failing community into a defensive side opposing negativity and elevating the mind to a purposeful level. I must say, there are many black men that are good for the black community, **but the truth is**: there are way too many black men that are also responsible for the demise of the black community and for the deaths of too many black youths.

The noose is not only symbolic to the many tragedies men, women, and children experienced in the past, but it also chokes hope out of the heart of those striving for a better tomorrow during this present time. The only difference is that the carrier of today's symbolical noose are young black men. How is it so? Because black men are the ones' suppressing the black community and largely in part, more than 70 percent of young black men that are dying in the streets aren't dying at the hands of white men, but they are being killed by other black men. This equates to tragedy.

As mentioned before, the same hope that was choked out years ago is the same hope that is lost when crime occurs in the streets throughout black community. So the question remains. WHERE ARE THE REAL BLACK MEN IN THE COMMUNITIES? Where are the black men that have made it out of the streets? Have they forgotten the pathways of difficult times, and constant struggles of the days of ole'? And do they not care to give back by helping to better educate other black males?

If my adjustments from wrong experiences doesn't cause me to liberate myself and educate another, it's only then that I've fail to realize the price it cost to be a MAN.

In order to arrive at the truth of why black youths invoke violence towards each other, we must first admit that black males are more prone to violence, and then ask ourselves, why? If we are to stand in truth we must ask: Are young black men really killing other black youths? If so, is there anyone to blame? If men within a drug infested or crime ridden community will not take a stand, does it mean the innocence of our children should continue to suffer at the hands of what black men fail to do? These are questions that black males have ran away from far too long. As long as black men continue to ignore the truth and escape their responsibilities by not being pillows in their communities and abroad, then black males will continue to see high rates of homicides.

While there are many that say the black community needs a leader in order to restore hope, I beg the differ. I believe that every young man that has the courage to stand, also have the ability to lead. The reasoning behind the failure to lead is secondary to how black males remove themselves from their responsibilities and when this is done, leading becomes impossible, especially when one busy himself by becoming a follower.

The search for leaders are not going to be found at the top level in society. Many of the black leaders that have a platform to speak out about the constant violence that black males invoke, refuse to do so because there is no money in saving black males. Not only is this unfortunate because it writes the tough truth about a group of males that sometimes refuse to be coached, but it shines the truth towards the real gain that is place upon the heads of the many black males that are frown upon from both sides.

My point and case, I have witnessed marches secondary to police brutality against black men. I have seen busloads of black leaders along with prominent black figures give up their family time and pursue trying to prevent racial hatred against black males. I have seen this time and time again, but when blacks kill blacks there are rarely any marches nor no bull horns or no shouting to stop the violence! Why is it? Is it because there is no money in saving black men from the destruction of themselves or is it because we only respond to the pain of the past?

Young black males as early as fourteen or fifteen can be shot down with high power rifles, robbed and shot for no reason at all, killed at house parties, and in the end, we seldom hear anything coming from the same leaders that seek the public's attention by way of the media when black males are harmed by the police.

If black males are to change and make a difference in the black community, there must be a response when any youth is killed and the horn should be blown each and every time. The murders of young black youths in which we read about day after day should be treated as if they were killed by the same ones in which many blacks are willing to march against. In other words, we have to starting marching on ourselves, for the pain we invoke upon ourselves.

Moreover, leaders must be made from the same young boys that are found standing on the corners looking to make a sell to their own culture of people. Those will be the young boys that are peddling the ideal of being a thug or gangster. The simple answer to this problem is that, people will empower people only if they are mentally awakened, and are willing to be empowered. Without this willingness to be empowered, it will ultimately close the doors for young men to realize their true potentials. The reason is because they are socialize to believe a lie by no one else but other black males who expresses negativity by way of violence, which creates the lie.

Anything else that exists aside from the truth of this matter has to be an element of denial, which is a dangerous experience to embrace.

What then would be the key to liberating a person from an environment that fights against itself? The answer is Education, Education, and even higher Education.

If one keeps the same mindset and feel they must stay true to the hood, then that mindset will continually be arrested by unforeseen circumstances that causes you to struggle, and never become acquainted with the potentials one have on the inside. Much of the potentials that you'll miss can be blamed on the manipulation of the environment. Therefore, black men must educate recessive minds, instead of destroying an already struggling environment. If this concept can't be visualized, then the blindness will only strengthen the noose that is already in place upon the black community.

Aside from this, one must learn how to release in order to increase. I'm speaking of increasing yourself in knowledge and establishing your mind with longevity and a reason for existing other than to go to jail or sell drugs. By standing in the doorway of open knowledge it will help release you from the confinements of a negative environment. Once this is achieved, it will not mean forgetting where you come from, but it means returning to help strengthen others by denying violence and dwelling in peace.

Finally, when you release yourself, this releasing

constitutes a realization of where you stand as a man, and most importantly, what you stand for. If you fall victim to the so called "selling –out" theory then, it is possible to be pulled in by the consequences of negative experiences that has ruined way too many black communities. This will leave you in a position that is seemingly unrealized and heavily flawed.

Black MANipulation

Ignorance will never know its presence in the company of good morals. Therefore, never practice it. christopher

Bestowed upon the minds of many black men, is the veil of being "misunderstood." This veil intertwines alongside the experiences of respect which should be found in every corner of a real man's life.

This misunderstanding introduces the experience of being black, how blacks are to conduct themselves, and the reasons behind self aggrandizement. On a different scale, there is another experience used commonly by many black males in which many hate to acknowledge. That is, too many black males strive to move upward in life off the shoulders of weaker black people. In other words, many are willing to continually devastate the lives of others, by selling drugs, robbing neighborhoods of their peace, imputing fear, and attempting to control limited territories for the temporary gain of self. This is manipulation.

I would like to paint a picture that can easily be identified, but if denial resides within you, it will never be recognized. So, he we go. For just a moment, try to identify the rough neighborhoods within your surrounding community. Now, what if there were no policemen or narcs patrolling these communities, what will happen? What if the policemen never responded to the drug sells, the prostitution, or the homicides that goes on day after day. What if no one responded when things are stolen, or people are robbed or shot at gun point? What do you think will happen? Now ask yourself, why is it that way too many black males seized the opportunity to destroy communities but refuse to be held responsible?   Aside from this, who are to be blamed for the despondency of ourselves, our children and our community? In order to reach and understand the truth which stands alone in the mind of every woman and man, we must first deny our own selfishness, and deal with what stands to be corrected within the corridors of our own hearts.

With that being said, being African American is a rich experience that is none like the experience of any other ethnic group in America. But, I have grown to realize that the negative experiences in which many subject themselves to on a day to day basis is uniquely found, and at the same time troublesome. In many cases, those experiences one may inherit from the streets are turned around and used against other blacks with a destructive nature in mind. This happens simply because many black men not only fail to respect other black men, but they fail to LOVE them as black men.

Those that call themselves gangsters, or thugs are also the same black men proclaiming to be pro-black.

Therefore, the question is now aimed at asking, whom are you thugging against?

Upon realizing this, some acknowledge a huge token of anti-peace which hangs within the hearts of those that are seen as unmade men. The reason this hangs there is secondary to the lack of character development that was never placed upon the developing minds of too many black males.

In this instance, life is cut short because of ignorance. This is consider unlearned and as long as young males continue to embrace such behavior like these, it will only perpetuate negative experiences by allowing more and more black males to become noosed.

For this purpose, many young and unlearned black males would quickly say "I love my black race" without considering the actions that may conflict with the words proceeding out of their mouth. Some will even stand up and protest for the improvement of the black race but never stand in the roles of being an effective leader or mentor, in the black community. It is there, where there is a dying need for more positive black men throughout every state in America.

On the contrary, based upon what we see and hear, there are many black men that have come out of good or disadvantaged backgrounds that are still rising up with an inclination to kill, rob, and destroy the very freedom in which many have died for, and many others refuse to live against.

In other words, if black males continue to dodge

higher education, consider themselves to be less valuable than they are, and procreate children without a desire to father them, then the violence we know today would only be the violence we will continue to see tomorrow, but on a larger scale.

This happens when young men lack the desire to be "released" and unknowingly this self containment will establish a negative legacy which will only imprison their potentials and prohibit the forward movement in life.

Youths that have found themselves at this cross walk seem to express it well. Once you fail to continue an upward and positive movement in life, it becomes enticing to seek pathways that will console your failures. Without doubt, one must realize that if you fail at something you have a wholesome desire for, it is not true failure unless you stop and refuse to stand up. But once you stand and begin to walk again, it germinates a tree of life.

Unfortunately, instead of improving self confidence by trying to find "the man" within yourself when you indulge in negative actions, many ultimately degrade and destroy their self worth by inviting negative proclivities to take the place of positive potentials.

These are the types of destructive tools that we see day after day, and unfortunately it has become a trait in which many black men themselves have accepted and are killing each other to prove their acceptance.

Finally, the unwillingness to deny that we (as black men) can be more dangerous to the black community when we superimpose this kind of danger and violence, is only the doorway entrance to manipulation. If black males continue such experiences like these it will always keep many blinded by the veil which has its' position in the doorway of the black mind.

Hanging for Respect

If I respect myself to any degree, then why would I put myself into the pathway of those who will bring me down?

If I respect my community, then why would I sell drugs to a damaged person in order to profit a temporary gain?

If I respect this life, then why would I seek to destroy something that I can never give back? The answer is simple. I have yet to learn the importance of RESPECT.
Christopher

In life, amongst the many positive tools one should acquire, this one particular tool is the most important. This acquisition will settle the issues of violence, manipulation, and unrest that has contaminated many black communities. This is the tool of respect for ourselves and respect for others. When men fail to realize that it is up to us as men to walk upright and extend the means to educate others, we then give way for trickery and manipulation. This happens when a negative surrounding is allowed to shape us into a position of failure

In regard to the respect of men, it is interesting to know that most, if not all men desire to be respected. Respect is that character trait that abides within the heart of every man. At any given time, it can extract itself according to the emotional experiences that are bound up on the inside of men.

Similarly, when respect is in its proper place, then understanding has its way of nurturing the finite mind. When understanding is embraced, then being able to apply it lays the foundation for knowledge to be recognized. If respect is to be carried upon the shoulders of young men with strong minds, then, this leaves little room for violence, or any other activity that brings the demise of young men.

On the contrary, *once respect is embedded within the hearts of both young and old men, they will then have the proper soil to produce a good growth of character.*

Aside from this, when positive attributes of the mind is replaced with the vulnerability of choosing a life of drugs, crime, or other sorts of violence, it is only then that respect becomes the failed experience one never took the time to embrace. The resulting experience is death or incarceration all because of the respect of character that was never in place.

With that being said, when one is incarcerated, being confined usually brings all things back to remembrance of how one should conduct themselves. But one must ask, why does it takes going to jail or prison? One of the young guys under my mentoring program was a perfect example. Despite all of the knowledge I imputed into him, he was still left to make a conscious decision on whether or not to do wrong.

Well, he went with his own decision which did not contain respect. Even though he could have called me at any time, said no to his negative associates, or simply spent the day at the library (in order to just think), he decided to commit a felony.

Now when he calls periodically from prison, all of a sudden he is aware of all the things he did wrong. This type of thought process becomes a very untrusting type of mindset, because it is usually their temporary confinement which makes them now behave the way they should have behaved in the first place. Unfortunately, the lesson is recognized in prison which is not too late, but does it take being locked up before some people would ever realize that they have the ability think?

In addition, not only should you be aware of your own thought process by allowing this to couple with the respect of self, but exercise your mind to increase mental strength   (reading, studying, etc.) and walk with the presence of respect. This gain of mental strengthening is definitely needed for black men, because too many young black children are attaching themselves to weaker vessels (thugs, drug dealers, etc.) and are being fed a false lifestyle by the people they should trust the most.

Comparatively, when I speak of vessels, I'm speaking of male youths, mentees, or some child that may not personally know you, but find themselves in the vicinity of your presence. They are all fragile young vessels awaiting to be strengthened.

If you are considered to be a strong and productive young man, your presence alone have the power to liberate minds that are entangled from the loopholes of selling drugs, gang banging or robbing. You must first acknowledge it before you can demonstrate it. This is what the beginning of leaving a legacy for those that follows will leave behind. God gave man the ability to shape, form, structure and strengthen not only self, but also the weaker ones we encounter.

Furthermore, if there is no challenging of "self," there will be no desire to search for ways to entrain proper knowledge, and **failure** becomes the result of your inabilities.

Having said that, when fathers go to jail for long periods of time, they usually leave behind their children and a loss sense of respect. The evidence of this seen time and time again throughout many communities signifies how respect is "hung" and someone must release the pressure from the slip knot, if there is going to be a change.

If we truly analyze how black males get into trouble, it's easy to assume that his selfishness is usually the reason for his mental imprisonment and this pain usually falls onto the family that is left behind. This pain weighs on the family financially and it goes something like this. The trouble of gathering up the money to go one's bond. The trouble of having to drive the distance to see fathers in prison. The high expenses impose upon families to talk to fathers from prison. And the pain of not having a dad around for that male advice. This goes on and on.

Experiences like these become stressors over time while trying to maintain communications with a father who decided to forsake everything underneath him all because he never understood respect of "self". And by the way, attorneys' fees and probation fees were never even added, but they can be incredible fees.

Onward, when respect is lost unto self, a noose is created. The primary purpose of the noose's creation by men is to provide a collapsing point in order to gain self fulfillment. When one overlooks himself with respect, he becomes dangerous to others, and rarely comprehend the extension of respect. When the noose is pulled onto a community and the slip knot collapses, death of the surrounding is always imminent. So, when we see the dealers on the corner, the pimps on the streets, and the gang bangers, we are witnessing the tightening of a noose upon the people within that community.

Furthermore, when communities are controlled and men within the communities have been destroyed by the use of drugs or some other device that controls their mind, then the experience of atrophy upon a community is initiated.

The meaning of atrophy relates to the complete wasting away of or part of the body. Think of the body as being the community. Atrophy occurs because men are not being used purposefully within the neighborhoods which leads to the wasting away of potentially strong men. Instead, there is more of an invitation to do negative and a desire to control their surrounding which can never happen, especially when atrophy can only begat weakness.

The long term effect of such an experience like this are the weaker minds that have failed to entrain the importance of education and self preservation. Instead, it is an invitation to fail. With this being allowed to happen, it slowly breaks down the social morals that can be found within people, until the pulse of life is weakened. Soon after, the community becomes pulse less.

After experiencing situations such as these, it becomes easy to point the finger at the existing situation. For example, many people blame the government, policemen, politicians, teachers, and everyone else except "self". Failure to recognize ones' own inadequate behavior is usually dealt with by pushing the blame in a different direction. When we see this occur, this is when we would know that *men have failed to become men.*

In a different light, the visibility of a disruptive community by way of criminal minds is strongly to blame for the failure of men. When this is understood, then self awareness will have us to become more of what we should become, rather than being what others make us stand as, secondary to dire circumstances within their surroundings.

Once again, the noose is not only symbolic to the many tragedies that men, women, and children experienced in the past, but it also chokes hope out of the heart of those striving for a better tomorrow in this present time. The only difference is that of the person holding the noose today and is causing mass murder of black males.

Onward, with the thousands of killings, robberies, and other activities that have robbed the black community of peace, I think it is fair to say that black men in the least, have done the greatest disservice to the black community. And the question still remains. WHERE ARE THE REAL BLACK MEN IN THE COMMUNITIES and why aren't they standing up?

Educate in Order to Liberate

If my adjustments from my wrong, doesn't cause me to liberate myself and educate another, then I've fail to realize the price it cost to be a MAN. christopher

The search for leaders are not going to be found at the top level in society. Leaders must be made from the same young boys that are found standing on the corners looking to make a sell. These are the young boys that are peddling the ideal of being a thug or gangster. In other words, people will empower people, only if the less empowered have the mind to become empowered. Without this continued empowerment and the opening of doors for young men to realize their potentials, a different door (the back door) will be open to receive those individuals that willingly overlook their opportunities.

What then would be the key to liberating a person from an environment that fights against them?.. Education...Education,.. Education.. If one keeps the same mindset that "you must stay true to the hood" then that mindset will continually be arrested by unforeseen circumstances which causes you to struggle. When this happens you rarely become acquainted with the true potentials you have on the inside. While growing up in the hood myself, it is one thing to leave the hood and seek better ways to increase one's understanding, but if you willingly accept a lifestyle which demonstrates self degradation, then this is consider foolishness.

Releasing yourself from the confinements of a negative environment does not mean forgetting where you come from, or selling out. These are terms or phrases

that are used to make one feel bad about their accomplishments Releasing yourself constitutes a realization of where you stand as a man, and most importantly, what you stand for. If you fall victim to the so called "selling –out" theory, then it's possible to be pulled in by the consequences of negative experiences, (selling, stealing, robbing, gang banging) and before long, instead of helping to overcome, one could fall victim to being overcame.

The Signature of Respect

Ignorance will never know its presence in the company of good morals. Therefore, never practice it.. christopher

Bestowed upon the minds of many, is the veil of being "misunderstood." This veil stands alongside the actions of respect, how one should give respect and how one receives it. For many years, this has been a complaint deriving from the black community, but I would like to focus on the understanding of respect and how it is deliver amongst the black community. This misunderstanding introduces the experience of being black, how black males should dwell amongst each other, and perhaps some reasons behind self aggrandizement.

Aside from this, those to blame for the despondency of that which finds itself pouring over our children and our community has to be aimed at those who stands in the shadows of leadership. In order to reach and understand the truth which stands alone in the mind of every man and woman, we must first deny our own selfishness, and deal with what stands to be corrected within reach of ourselves. The hope that we carry as black men can only be of significance when we work at the positives we strive to maintain, and neglect to destroy the black communities for selfish gain.

Having said that, the African American heritage is a rich experience that is none like the experience of any other ethnic group in America. However, I have grown to realize that some experiences in which many blacks go through on a day to day basis is uniquely found, but at the same time troublesome if we truly acknowledge the relationships that black males possess and their actions upon their community.

In many cases, there are too many negative experiences that are learned from the streets which are turned around and used against other black Americans with a destructive nature in mind. Is it because blacks don't respect blacks and don't see much hope in us ever changing, or is it because too many black males minimize their own self worth and continue to use the community as a hostile place to further commit terrorism?

Unbeknownst to the many people whom I have heard recite comments like these, they never realize what is expected of "self". This in return, closes the doors for many to make an analysis of self, and also minimizes the worth of self while denouncing the signature of respect for other people.

In all, true judgment starts with "self" by asking, how do I look, how do I feel, and what positive experiences do I plan to achieve at this time in my life.

In a way that is non-identical to how other races view us, the foundation of how blacks perceive blacks can sometimes be perceive as a greater negative based upon the violence we see day after day being committed against each other. For example, the many young black men that called themselves gangsters are the same black men that consider themselves to be pro-black when the call to march is implemented. In other words, if you proclaim to love your black race, and will stand up for the black race, then how does one take part in destroying their own community, and target to kill the same black males they struggle with through life. This is more of a pre planned ambition to impute a signature of "no respect" aimed directly back into the black community by no one other than black men.

Another example follows. Many want to be hustlers but who are they hustling? Are they really hustling someone else, or are they the ones being hustled by the penal system after committing crimes against their own. To even take on the mind set of hustling, one may suggest that the indifference some may have on their own community is more of an acceptance to be "ghetto" than it is to be socially good.

This is the kind of destructive tool that we see day after day, and unfortunately it has become a trait many blacks have accepted and are at times unwilling to deny.

From time to time, after researching and reading so many stories of black youths robbing and killing on the streets of America, it is hard to deny the very truth that stands in front of us. Furthermore, the unwillingness to deny that black men have been more dangerous to the black community in the last forty years than any other crucifying experience is a reality we have conformed to. The failure to realize this simple truth will always keep us blinded by our own experiences and the failure to respond in a positive and constructive way, can only continually damage black children that are being raised within a community led by black males with no desire to show respect.

Another example of how black men have failed to demonstrate respect is seen right in our community barbershops, where kids frequent all the time. At times when I'm sitting in the barber shop waiting to get a haircut for me or my sons, I usually entrain almost every conversation that is going on. Because most of the people in the barbershop are grown men, there should always be a certain type of atmosphere one wishes to control when kids are within the surrounding environment. Well, on many occasions the conversations aren't controlled. It never fails that there would be a man or two within those four walls that willingly curse every other sentence as if kids aren't listening. It never dawns on the assailant that kids are around and they talk how they like because they have no respect of self, or respect of people.

The same holds true for pickup basketball games. Usually the courts are in close proximity to some park where kids go to have fun. Unfortunately, while trying to have fun, there will always be two or three men out on the court that has no respect for anyone not even little kids. Why does this occur? Once again, the number one reason is ignorance, followed by a lack of respect. If respect is not planted within their hearts, then their convictions alone will never bring about the source of correction.

Having said that, if we as black men can recover ourselves away from the theory of being victimized and pay more attention to our "self made character," then we can detect the faults that lie within ourselves.

I have read countless stories where neighborhood drug dealers have not only sold within the community for years, but these same black men create violence or murder within the community the so-call protect, but ultimately destroy.

After the creation of such bad experiences like these, it challenges the mind and intellect of the neighbors that willing tolerate actions like these without standing up, even if they have to stand alone. Aside from this, if the law enforcements who are patrolling black neighborhoods seek to prevent drug sales, drug use etc. somehow ends up harming an individual of the same community, this will spark an outright civil rights march. My point is this: Couldn't the same neighbors that are now marching against the system, do an about face, and march against the drug dealers that are destroying the same neighborhoods daily with the use and sell of drugs and violence? Is this respect or is this blind obedience?

If black males are not willing to acknowledge what it means to walk in respect, and demonstrate better character, then the problem throughout the communities will continue to perpetuate and the murders of young black males will continue to rise.

Besides, during the years of analyzing the absolute truth concerning those issues which hurt black males, I come to conclude that the loss of respect for one can become contagious enough to create a greater loss for many.

On the contrary, in regards to respect of men, it is interesting to know that most, if not all men desire to be respected no matter what the case may be. Desiring respect is that one trait that abides within the heart of men and when it's rejected, the loss can be cumbersome and the unwillingness to forgive is sometimes the struggle that destroys a youth's life. This occurs because respect is usually projected according to the emotional experiences that are bound on the inside of us. Without it, trying to understand our heart's conviction can obscure our view. A continuation of this is how respect is usually carried around in silence, but it has the possibility of growing during moments of confrontation. For some, when respect is not admonished, they are willing to kill. But on the other hand, if you murder someone secondary to not respecting you, it's likely you'll end up in a place where many more are willing to disrespect you by any means. Right? So, why not establish control and initiate respect within yourself? If you really consider carrying out violence onto another person, every thought that blooms up in you will deal with some form of disrespect towards the receiving person(s).

Without saying, your character is quickly minimized the moment you become disrespectful, and in many cases you are the last to know.

Respect is also elusive, and it flows as swift as the wind. Respect has no one particular person to settle upon, but it is embraced by all that is willing to receive it. Unfortunately, the number of killings and drug distribution has pushed aside the respect in which many black women and black children should be receiving, but the lack thereof have left many unaligned black men looking away from what they should be taking a stand on. This stance is God, self, family, and neighbors. When this order is followed, respect for another will be able to pierce through the most callous experiences of life, regardless of the situation or the circumstances. If you search for good character you will find respect, and if you never extend it, it will be difficult to receive it from anyone else.

As most people already know, respect also has a pathway that is birth within the home. Being that the home is the foundation of it all, the pattern should flow from the home, into the schools, and from the schools, into the world. Most of the time when we witness young black men caught up in triumph, (murder, robbery, violence, etc.) these issues are all misaligned from the pathways mentioned above.

I can't tell you how many times, I've seen or witness guys getting beat up or even killed all over someone looking at them the wrong way. Think about this!!

Someone looked at you or your boy the wrong way, and now you decide to make them pay the consequences for staring at you. That sounds foolish right? This is the epiphany of not only ignorance that has lingered on too long among too many young men, but in the end, you will never receive true respect by igniting violence.

If you as a young man find yourself participating in practices like these, you will find yourself not only disrespecting who you are as an individual, but also disrespecting your family by bringing shame on them. In the end, the only person that will pay for the actions of ignorance *is he that stands in the shadow of it.*

Next, on a level that deals with respect for the community, when we fail to deny that many of our black communities are under arrest primarily by black drug dealers and gang bangers, we open the gate way of denial and start dwelling within a lifestyle that appears to be comfortable. In other words, we not only lose respect for ourselves, but we lose respect for the community.

With this continuing, failing to account for your actions as a man will not only fail the community when you involve yourself in destructive behavior but you ultimately arrest yourself without awareness. Once you arrest yourself subconsciously, it is hard to bond yourself away from what you feel is right, even though your actions are dead wrong. By doing this, it can easily prevent liberation from negative experiences and the whole myth of denying the ideal of what respect entails, will then become the experience you will struggle to overcome.

Lastly, as a young man, you should always acknowledge who you are, where you stand, and consistently take part in positive contributions starting within your family and migrating outward into the communities. This is how Respect is demonstrated!

If you put respect for yourself and others on board in your life, it will change how you perceive your life in its entirety. Then, once you open your eyes to the truth concerning your surroundings, it become easy to abide with respect because it will then have a platform.

The Strength of Respect

When I desire to be stronger, I delve into myself and create a stronger sense of respect for myself. Only then, am I stronger.   Christopher

How does one discover their strengths and deliver it as respect? Strength is not found in fighting nor is it found in your home boys. The only way to find a solidified strength is to acknowledge the "respect" that is waiting to be release deep down on the inside of you. If you never practice walking with respect and giving it away to others, then you will never own it, and acknowledging it is difficult to come by. In comparison, when respect has no place in the heart of a man, then fear has a way of overwhelming him to compensate for what he otherwise fail to produce. Respect.

In the book called Restoring Hope by the great educator Professor Cornell West, Maya Angelou makes this statement during an interview. " he doesn't know he's already been paid for. But he (black men) walks down the street as if he has oil wells in his backyard." This statement is overwhelmingly powerful and it depicts the direct truth in how many of many black males walk through life.

Many young black men don't understand where

they came from, nor who died for them, hence the reason why many misunderstand the shadows they stand in today. Ask yourself these questions. Why would you drop out of high school when so many people gave their lives for you to have a better education? Or, why would you involve yourself in doing something that would place you in jail? Does your freedom not mean anything to you?

Over the years, the number of black males that have been murdered by other black males all have one thing in common. The one thing that many fail to acknowledge is the token of respect that is found within the individual. Without this acknowledgement, it leads to the inability to walk in a respectful way. Many of the homicides that I have followed throughout the country either involved drugs, robbery or some type of beef that was going on between two or more people and the overwhelming amount were men that lack respect for themselves and or their community.

In reality, if you analyze each one of these experiences, you can pin point exactly where the trait of respect was abused, or for some, never embraced at all.

It is one thing to have respect for your mother, father (for some), grandmother, close relatives or even your homeboys. But the respect I'm speaking of, is the type of respect that is extended easily without barriers or attitude that will misalign your character no matter who it is that stands before you.

If this is overlooked, these concerns will not only

destroy the character of young men alike, but will also minimize their level of maturity, because males have a need to feel respected. Without a shadow of a doubt, if black males are to understand their surroundings they must also understand the concept of respect. This must be realized because the only place for anger to dwell when it has no boundaries is within "you".

In truth, your biggest job in formulating your character should involve cultivating your thoughts, preserving the goodness of "self", and expressing it unto others. When you express deformation of your character, you automatically lose the battle with respect. The reason is secondary to the overlooked issues within the primary individual. If you are preventing this experience from coming to life by misrepresenting the jewel that you have on the inside, then it will never pierce through those dark moments nor illuminate your character, or your attitude.

The strength of respect provides a pathway that illuminates the ability to stand alone and allow others to judge you based upon what they see. If you decide to stand against walking in respect, then it's hard to convince anyone of your positive traits and this have been a break down for many young males.

When you initiate respect within yourself, it will be hard for other young males to approach you with a plan that will ultimately ruin your life. One thing to remember is this. When ignorance is bound on the inside of wayward minds, it will always look for others to identify or couple with along that downward pathway.

Furthermore, when you embrace respect within yourself, it would never allow you to go around pulling a gun out on anyone. Therefore, when you respect yourself it will never make sense to sell drugs, or gang bang. But without respect, you give way to ignorance because ignorance stands the chance to run parallel with violence simply for the sake of losing respect instead of gaining it.

The youths that I have mentored were always taught to respect "self" first. Some perceive respect as something that is predicated upon what one looks like, what someone drives, how they act (negatively), or even where they come from. None of these things hold true weight in defining respect. As a young man, if you feel like you should give respect to another young man secondary to his actions, especially when they are meaningless, then you are failing to understand your own strengths. So, if you fail to understand your own strengths, you then walk around with weakness, and this weakness leads to the inability to STAND.

To look at it differently, respect doesn't have a face. Respect doesn't have a certain voice but it is known to last even after the life of those that left a legacy of positive experiences. When one looses respect, someone or something is always disrespected. When one loose respect, changes occur and sometimes it can never be adjusted to fill the void of that which is left behind. Respect is earned and the way you present yourself to the world will be the way you are usually judged once you leave this world. This is the power of RESPECT.

Like anything else, respect can be channeled in its own direction, but you must be willing to control the will of your character in order for others to acknowledge what you stand for. Ultimately, you will either care about what you do and receive a good token of respect or not care and have your consequences be controlled by the law.

With the continual stripping of respect and the killing of young black males, the family unit will continue to weaken and soon the foundation of what we know as the black family will be no more. If the core of a problem have a weak foundation, then that foundation will remain fragile until it is supported in a stabilized way. This weak foundation that I'm referring to is the displacement of young black men.

When black male fathers displace themselves, it gives their children difficult pathways to choose and many end up living a life "in search of" rather than living a life with direction. Too many have also sewn their seeds in many different areas causing an unstable foundation and the misalignment of many families. Unfortunately, too many black women have accepted this wavering type of behavior in which black men have displayed. This type of behavior within its own right invites the type of disrespect that many women are unfortunately willing to except, and for bizarre reasons, many black women embrace. For example, out of the negative experiences of disrespect, we hear such phrases like "My baby's daddy." This has become such a common phrase, that to embrace such phrases like this seemingly incarcerates the level of mentality and questions one's maturity and even their spiritual and moral character.

At times, what seems so natural to embrace culturally, can sometimes end up being a tool of suppression, all because we never took the time to analyze some of the negatives we quickly embrace.

Overall, to find strength within a culture, one can test the vessels (men) of any community and find strength wherever good men take a stand. If the men are weak, then, one must empower the weaker vessels with the might to believe in themselves, and the security of knowing that success is birthed when impregnated with passion and desires.

But on the other hand, to defeat a culture of people, one must only mimic the negatives in which they live amongst. This mimicking is established to further create manipulation. If you create manipulation within any culture with the mindset of loving the very ones you actively seek to destroy, then and only then will that culture defeat itself from within. This happens because it (culture) remains blind to what it has learned to embrace (unlearned black men).

To confuse and destroy a culture, one can distort the perception of the people from what they can become, causing them to think that they are not their own enemies. However, the question remains: Would an enemy or friend sell the community drugs, or violence only to keep them hostage unto themselves and create a breakdown of values within its own environment? Answer: only enemies would do this.

During the month of February 2012, a home invasion took place in the city of

Atlanta, Ga. During this home invasion, six black men entered into the home of another seeking to take control over something that they could never control, another person's property. During this home invasion, in which all of them were black, ranging from the ages in the high teens into the 40's, they chose to shoot a fifteen year old honor roll and football star student in the chest. Their negligence, their ignorance, and their unlearned minds took the life of an innocent kid. Not only was this tragic, but it sheds the light upon the strong ignorance that criminal mind black males take part in against their own race, leaving others to wonder if it will ever stop.

Ruining an Education to Run the Community

At one point and time in my life, I was on the edge of thinking that others were out to minimize who I was within this world. While growing up as a teenager, I recalled being told by so many black men that "the white man ain't going to give you nothing." I heard this phrase so many times that I started to believe it. But as I grew older, I realized that most of the homicides, robbery, and violence came by way of my own people. I became dismissive of the fact that I was held down by the system. Had I continued to be misinformed and never realized my true potentials, I would have held myself back from a world of opportunities. C.S.

In the state of Georgia alone, the graduation rate stated in 2007 was under 50%. The question becomes, who is to blame? The number of teen violence and gang violence display signs of increasing death rather than decreasing death rates. To blame the school system for not obtaining a good education is one thing, but to blame the school system for the lack of morals or character that our young men display is absurd. Aside from this, when kids drop out of school, where do they go? Who do they affect? And what do they accomplish?

In order for any problem to be resolved, there must

be an area of focus that must be identified and corrected by all means. For far too long, that problem has been at the doorstep of displaced black men and their abandonment from themselves and families. When black men neglect themselves, this neglect comes by way of minimizing their ability to be informed, dropping out of school, infiltrating communities with manipulative ideals, and holding down drug ran corners.

Starting at the level of the family, if love, strength, and a pattern of consistency is not implemented onto each child, we then witness a growth in which we as parents can partly be responsible for ensuing. If unconcerned black men continue to give the government the power to implement plans for disobedient black youths, then their plan would always go something like this:

For those young males that refuse to learn, and have no desire to extend good moral skills, then the government will continue to build more prisons. **The truth is**: The government by no means, is interested in rearing what it did not produce. The government is not responsible for going out and making babies, therefore, they will not take part in raising them. Neither is the government responsible for robbing or killing black males, therefore, it will only be right to restrain those that are causing harm unto others or abusing the rights of other citizens.

Continually, when our kids step out of the boundary of respect, there is a covering that is lost.

When we become uncovered we give up who we truly are, and what we can truly become. I've seen prominent neighborhoods dilapidate down to a state of violence and drugs and the number one reason is due to the loss of covering. The covering of a community is symbolic of the respect in which people should walk in, display amongst each other, and distribute from one unto the other. This covering is taught and reared by the BLACK MAN.

Nowadays, when I'm out riding through neighborhoods, that were once striving neighborhoods, I notice young men hanging on corners, and or walking up and down the streets with white or black T-shirts on. Some can make the argument that there is nothing wrong with our young boys wearing baggy pants and T's, but these are the ones that are blind to the serious issues that are plaguing the black community. Similarly, the same formulated groups that was atone time innocent, has now become a gang related issue. Remember. *To remain numb to such issues, will only give strength to the negativity of an uncovered environment.*

The truth goes something like this. Throughout the many areas in the black community, we can clearly see what our own problems are but lack the experience or heart to tackle issues that have become commonly accepted. On a similar note, when one judges him or herself on the grounds of moral character, it is more difficult to believe the truth about ourselves, especially if we are surrounded by destructive individuals.

Aside from this, we sometimes second guess our own potentials and look for a greater reason to fall, secondary to what is perceived as good. The reason behind this is simple. For many, failing to take a stand may sometimes challenge a person against their own inability to rise up. Ask yourself this question. How many young black men do you see in a days' time that walk the neighborhoods and streets trying to make a sell, or get ahead in life, by way of doing something against the law? If people within the community started calling the police each time someone came through trying to sell drugs, clothes or items they have stolen, then cops wouldn't be able to police the criminals fast enough. This is the magnitude of hopelessness that too many black men have implemented onto their own people.

Too many of us have become so immune to the wrong that goes on daily, that most look away and accept the corruption, which ultimately grows into destruction. Witnessing situations like these are the number one signs that we have lost respect not only for our neighbors, but for the community as a whole. The numbers are huge, and as young boys grow up to witness similar looking young men with negative behaviors, then the fight to overcome that resistance (negative behavior) will continue to distort their view on what a black man should truly be like.

Hanging the Image

What is found in an image? Some forms of image is predicated upon how one is perceived or how one looks by way of dress attire. Image is a form of communication that will present itself unto the sense of sight, as well as tread the inner walls of trust vs. non trust.

When we witness this generation of kids walking around with oversized shirts, pants, gold teeth, and dreads, the majority of these kids are in search of character. While in search of character, they are trying to identify themselves within a world while being misled down a pathway that is uncertain. This is not just a style called "hip hop", but it's an accepted way of social denigration through the lack of understanding.

The whole idea of dressing this way seems so accepted and harmless that kids (especially black kids) buy into this way of denigrating imagery without giving it a second thought. This type of attire inflicts a red mark upon their character and sometimes their personality when neither is unknown by others. And this appearance allows others to judge you based upon the norms of social morality not what you are trying to look like.

For the most part, as we walk along the pathways of this world, we are judged based upon several things.

One of those things that we are judged on is called "image." The first mental note one takes when meeting someone new, is their appearance. What they look like? What are they wearing and sometimes, why are they wearing it? Whenever we meet anyone for the first time, it is natural as humans to take a mental application on what is before us. We then mentally register a note to either trust or not trust that image that is before us.

In all essence, what you appear to be or look like usually pours the foundation for what your inner characteristics will hinge upon. When young men fail to fill these important shoes in life, then their struggle for hire will continue to be an issue.

I'm bringing this to the forefront of your thoughts because most young men walking around with their pants hanging low are essentially walking out of character, but are unaware of it. In doing so, many of them are removing themselves from having more than what they could have all because they lack the understanding of grooming their appearance. With that being said, many walk with the attitude of "you can't tell me what to wear", but thinking this way creates self defeat and keeps you at a low place in society.

Alongside the previous statement, what you acknowledge in life is what you sometimes stumble over. By realizing your self-confidence, when you present yourself to the world it will only birth enlightenment and overshadow the unknown that is usually adopted by others. Your presentation to others outside of your family circle will ultimately be the ones you will have to market yourself unto for the rest of your life and your image will have a big influence on whether people will embrace you or deny you.

I use the word market, because the world itself is a marketing platform. We all walk on this platform and are scrutinized to some degree by each and everyone that we encounter. Our encountering with other people helps to create opinions that resonate throughout the mind and places us in a position to be scrutinized. These formulated opinions are something we all have a right to negate from or embrace. But unlike our own opinions, other people opinions have to be respected if our character is flawed. In the end, you only hurt yourself and place yourself at a greater disadvantage when competing for jobs.

Many of our teenage young men that are walking around trying to depict a certain image, usually carry this same type of image into their twenties. I have even seen thirty and forty year old men walking around with their pants "sagging." The truth is: Many just have not grown up and realized that their presentation unto the world is usually how the world presents itself back. If you choose to look like nothing and carry yourself like nothing, then chances are, you will be limited to having nothing. This goes for jobs, schools, peers, and others that may play an intricate part in whether you move upward or down life.

Lastly, the truth (of who you are characteristically)

will never fail to present itself, unless "self" closes its mind and never receive it. When young men hang their images they also hang their characters. This may not make sense to them given their youthful mind and their lack of wisdom. But when walking through denigrating experiences like these, it sometimes gives an uncertain mind the need to belong to something whether positive or negative.

Over a period of time, one can easily find himself in a dilapidated state of mind, if you allow your appearance to creep in and affect not only what you look like, but even what you behave like. Along with an adverse effect with this kind of negative behavior, follows irresponsibility.

This is another thing that kills many unlearned minds over and over. For example, not being responsible enough to say no to joining gangs or not being responsible enough to stand up and remove yourself away from the negative crowd. Some say it's peer pressure, but I call it standing against the pressure and seeking to be lead into chains.

Overall, you must realize that you are who you are primarily by how you present yourself to others as a young man. Some of my mentees complain of being judged while going out on different job interviews. I am always challenging them to bring that which is on the inside, outwardly, and wear it on the outside. If you feel like you are a champion on the inside, then why not wear it on the outside by displaying how you feel on the inside.

Like any and everything else we could visibly see, all things have forms of communication. If you are walking around, with your legs wide open because your pants are almost on the grown, this clearly depicts a sign of laziness and irresponsibility. No matter how you look at it, the way you allow *yourself* to walk around, is the way you will be perceived. The same holds true for those walking around with gold grills, seeking to command attention, with hopes that somebody will recognize them. This type of nonverbal communication says: "I don't have a high opinion about what I look like." In other words, my self esteem is low and my "character" is following in the direction of where my pants are hanging at, and that's downward.

Even more, it has become more than a challenge to reach a number of young black men once they adjust to this life style. The challenge is secondary to the lack of understanding their own character and how they easily seek to copycat other's character. Just simply ask the question sometimes. Why are your pants sagging? Why are you wearing a shirt four times your size? Why? Their answer is usually never clear, because they really can't give you a good reason for it. When you forsake the good of your own character, your morals and integrity will also be forsaken. Without a shadow of doubt, your image can be described as the skirt that overlaps you morals and integrity. Standing next to these two is the expression of dignity which position itself to be expressed outwardly. So, when you bundle them all together, it become the synapses of yourself worth which is a big source of strength given by God.

When you disregard what you look like and prohibit the learning of good teaching, it is then that you inadvertently introduce yourself to a theory of self defeat. Self defeat deals with the ideal of destroying your character before your character is ever made. In other words, don't destroy yourself before you make yourself. This usually happens during the preteen and teenage years. If this is allowed to go on unchecked, then by the time you are twenty you would have already cemented your feelings based upon what you feel you should look like in public.

Many also inadvertently destroy their characters before they reach adulthood. Once they have walked the pathway of being a thug, or weed head, it becomes difficult for them to turn themselves around due to the emotional connection they have established with what they are trying to appear to be in life. This is what I call the *addiction to life afflictions.*

Moreover, this type of attitude or image of self defeat makes it difficult for young men to move along the pathway of improving their livelihood. Instead they run into dead ends, and feel inadequate and this leads them to give up on life. By doing so, multiple struggles are placed upon family members as some fight to save their sons from prison or the grave yard.

The truth is: If you have plans on moving up in life, we all have to change something within and about ourselves to make ourselves more marketable for the real world. Usually that change involves attitude and character. Image is also an experience of change that must be realized in order to fulfill a purposeful destiny. Image is elusive and sometimes farfetched to the point of being senseless in the eyes of some (depending on what you're trying to look like) but most of all, image personifies a directive pathway to truth. Furthermore, the experience that you walk in from day to day not only brings into view an individualized judgment factor of self, but also cross cultural boundaries. In doing so, your image give others a small view of your world, and sometimes your best look will carry you through.

Image is also a powerful force to be reckoned with and a spiritual force that is sometimes difficult to understand. Who you say you are verbally is one thing, but your reflections, which are carried out before the world puts the seal on defining you as a person. With all due respect to image, it can somehow become the author of your present being and tells the story behind the reflections of your character. I have known numerous young men whom have tried to convince me to overlook their sagging clothes and acknowledge their intellect. But unbeknownst to most of them, a person's intellect automatically becomes secondary to an "image." Learning to care about what you look like on the outside will influence others of how you are on the inside.

In other words, once you enlarge your thinking

capacity and start to visualize with your mind, rather than dress down your image, then that existing will redirect you to an altitude where wisdom will dress up the inner flaws and your outer appearance will benefit from it.

Moreover, trying to convince one of your intelligence while looking like a bum, would only suggest that your desires in life are misaligned from where your mind and heart is trying to go. Needless to say, the thug image has brought under arrest the minds of too many young men who are not aware of the black mark they place upon their character when they walk around "sagging or bagging."

For the most part, many feel no self conviction because of the established acceptance they have embraced towards a life style that looks worthless but feel discriminated against when descent jobs turn a blind eye. But the question is, how does an individual blame others for recognizing, what they themselves fail to recognize?

Meanwhile, those individuals that are insecure of their inner self will automatically annihilate those inner convictions, in order to stand against what appears to be right. Some young men even reach the point of feeling funny when they wear something that is nice and appropriate, because it stands against their emotions and their character they have been developing all the long. This is how strong image or appearance can affect a person.

The continuation of this thugged out image must be

destroyed in order to bring forth a more true identity, and more desirable potentials. In order to turn away from looking and feeling like a thug, you must deny yourself from dressing inappropriately (which they feel is nothing wrong with), talking foolishly, and walking inaccurately through a society which judges from all angles. Once again, you are your greatest asset unto yourself. Some can do this with ease, but others struggle intrinsically to appear in a way that expresses decency and rarely deny the onslaught of indecency.

One must also realize that your image is the key expression to your personal identification label. Having said that; it is only when you are in search of an identity that one should express positive attributes. When this is done, one can only liberate the mind of those that have no directions in life. But if you walk against the truth of your inner self, then this image of sagging, grilling, and mean mugging, will never allow you to challenge your character to its' fullest potentials. When this happens, mental imprisonment becomes the cave that many find it difficult to escape from, and it generally relates to the creation of a false image.

In the aftermath, there must be a mental an awakening of black youths if there is to be correction. For this to occur you must realize your worth and have a desire to become, instead of a desire to never be. On the contrary, one must wonder why young males are willing to denigrate themselves by way of what they look like and what they refuse to do? The answer is simple. A weak mind can never see past the things that are before them.

Through our walk in life, we sometimes search for outer things that hold value, but forget to search within ourselves to bring forth those values that are truly meaningful. Furthermore, there are many young people without direction in life who end up falling victim to such experiences like these because they rarely discover themselves because reject themselves.

In conclusion, if young men are to become thinkers and doers, they must have an opened mind to receive knowledge deeper than street level knowledge. This image of looking thuggish and sagging pants will always suppress those true inner qualities that are found within the individual. To say the least, our dressed up image in which we put on from day to day is either for our own appeasement or for the sake of grasping the attention of others. But if we fail while trying to impress, we must remember that our walk and our talk in life is what really put us in the spot light to be judged.

In Search of Change

I decided to write this chapter because I wish to bring to the fore front the truth about what we sometimes dismiss about our black culture. I found it easy to speak of the truth concerning problems in the black community. The reason is because it is much easier to blame an institution or entity that once suppressed us rather than swallow the blame ourselves and hold ourselves accountable for what we fail at accomplishing. Coupled with this reasoning is the desire to blame others for our own shortcomings, especially when we fail to see and achieve during our moment of blindness.

In many cases, our actions speak for itself. What we do unto each other will always run parallel unto what others will do unto us at some point in our lives. However, when the truth about "self" is dismissed, it is only then that we begin to search for those that share a common interest in order to validate our own short comings or activities of demonstrating our own level of inadequacy.

While in search of the truth, change may never occur for some, because sometimes it's better to accept flawed characteristics rather than push back the truth and strengthen the individual "self".

Consequently, when negative proclivities becomes a

part of who you are as an individual, it becomes a difficult task to change, especially if you remain closed minded to what truth entails and how your emotions can sometimes be elusive. This type of mental incarceration will always cause one to minimize the truth.

Because of this, the reason behind the minimization of the truth then becomes secondary to what unmade men remain incapable of doing, and how they will use their surroundings to further denigrate the lives of others and themselves. In other words, black men that are ruining the black communities will never see the negative part of the whole picture. The reason: Because a shaded heart will always have a difficult time when standing in the presence of innocence, and the negative roles that are played will always be dismissed in their minds. In short, when you can find the means of why you do what you do, you will also find a reason to justify it.

When the truth about a culture is dismissed, then over a period of time complacency will soon over-shadow the strengths of the people and weakness will have its' way of displaying a picture that finds itself incomplete.

The problem with being dismissive about community violence, drugs and robbery, is that it invites us to look within ourselves and observe a cloudy picture of what we as blacks tolerate from each other and how we tolerate those things around us. At times, this is hard to accept. But by acknowledging that change must occur, it can birth an experience of understanding and unfold the pathway of peace and longevity.

The understanding of knowing that, the very thing that blacks once fought to be liberated from, has now become the one thing that many black men refuses to stand up for. The name of that experience we sometimes refuse to stand for is called, Change.

In order for change to occur one must invest within his self in order to change negative proclivities in which placates the mind, and prohibits intellectual growth. Many young boys that are on the streets will always find it difficult to change because they have placed their emotions into something that is emotion less. This emotionless atmosphere is called their "negative environment". With that being said, many black youths manipulate themselves to think they must act a certain way in order to coexist within a particular environment, when in truth this type of coexistence only leads to the destruction of rival black males and the reasons for murder can never be justified. This type of behavior also leads to our young black males developing a negative behavior against other black males while true love is minimized.

I have also come to realize that if anything will cause a culture or group of people to collapse, it will be the people (themselves) within that particular group. Here is the reason: *When outside opposing forces seek to destroy or bring a group of people down, the elements of unity arises within that group, and temporarily, those unforeseen issues are pushed aside. Thereafter, "the right to protect" becomes visibly dominant. But when a group of people choose to overlook devastating issues that are eliminating or imprisoning their own, then, destruction will have its rightful place within that very same group. This destruction is due to the lack of knowledge not being utilized and inflicted pain that goes unnoticed amongst the stronger vessels within that community.* That stronger vessel is the Black Man.

On a different note, your life in its entirety can only be lived out by you and your walk along the pathway in this world can only be walked by you. The ultimate decision based upon whether or not you should commit an act of crime or not, is totally up to you. These are the basic levels of understanding "self", because in the end it will be "self" that is left to suffer any and all consequences.

Prior to dealing with your own actions, you must note; that before you walk into unforeseen circumstances, you must first THINK!! I can guarantee you that more than the majority of criminals that are serving time in jail wish they could have another chance now that they are confined and have the time to think. If they had a second chance, I'm sure they would tell you what they would have done different. Some can't have that second chance because they lost their lives during the negative activity they were involved in.

At this point, this is where the doors open up for you to review the experiences of those you may have known or read about in the newspapers, or even seen on the evening news. So, without doubt always remain positive and the influence that you gain will be contagious to others.

The Mind to Change

It is during those times of hardship, that real men should impart morals, positive behavior and good character, regardless of the environmental circumstances. For example, you may dwell in a bad environment, but you don't have to join a gang or smoke dope to fit in with those that are walking towards an early death. In truth, when you give in to following such negativity, that weakness in which you fail to realize about yourself maybe the very reason you are killed or jailed at an early age. This is why it pays for you to know who "you" are in life, and where you are going before others assist in minimizing your position in life without any regards to what you stand for.

If you desire to change the position from where you are in life now, and move to where you desire to be in life later on, then, there must be an awakening of self. If "self" is not awakened then dreams dissipates, becoming the nightmare which turns into a reality that only "you" will have to deal with.

I have a friend by the name of Greg who spent time in jail for shooting two other young men. Greg was and still is one of my best friends. During the time that Greg and his cousin Tony put themselves into that stressful situation, and ended up shooting these guys, they were in an environment that was too hostile. The good thing is that no one died.

After going to jail, Greg spoke of the nights that he would wake up thinking that his being in prison was simply a dream. Unfortunately, it was not a dream. He would wake up in a jail cell, and each day that he spent there, he knew that prison was not a place for him. To say the least, it took Greg's going to jail in order for him to realize what he should have easily known before hanging in the wrong place and with the wrong type of people.

This was a case of lacking the ability to identify with "self." When you forget to identify with yourself, those unlearned experiences will make you pay for what you fail to learn, when you step into the experiences of trouble. There are too many young black men that are in prison, because they never knew their true potentials nor identified with what they could become. In many ways they only became what the environment, or some other negative influence allowed them to become, because they never fought to change their "mind."

It should never be your purpose to walk around carrying a gun. It shouldn't be your purpose to join up with a group of thugs that will never go anywhere in life. Living a life in this manner can never be purposeful, but it can be considered foolishness and foolishness will always be in conflict with a true purpose. Your true search starts with being able to identify with the "real" you and dismiss what others wish to make you.

If one wishes to create foolishness instead of success, then by all means, keep denying yourself the right to succeed. Foolishness can never lead into your gold mine of potentials if you remain in darkness. Pathways like these are just barriers in life that will restrict you from pulling out the good that is within you, and prevent you from making good use of your potentials by overwhelming you with negative attachments in your life.

Therefore, if you wish to fail in life, just remember that it is very simple, and *it doesn't take much accomplishing anything in life, especially if you wish to achieve nothing.*

Furthermore, self awareness would also be the ticket to who you decide to get on board with. When the truth about "self" is unknown, it then allows unknown circumstances to control you, leaving you in search of a way out from the negative issues created. You then move from not wanting to learn anything in this free society, to having criminals (guys in jail) teach you the basics on law, in order to liberate you from what physically contains you. This is the awakening that many black male are confronted with when sent to prison.

This reality of spending time away is the reason why one must search within the confinements of self. By searching yourself, it introduces you to a philosophical understanding of who you are and the reason for your existence. But before reaching a point of physical imprisonment, it is imperative to understand that everyone has a chance at succeeding without first having to lose their freedom. If you overlook this small but needed experience in your life, you will always kneel to weakness along with those that have kindred spirits like yourself.

Without a changed mind, it will also be difficult for the individual that is falling in life to take a "stand" especially if he is supporting other individuals that are headed in a similar direction. If you already struggle with the desire to change from bad to good, then the only way change will come is when you are made to change. That is, if you refuse to change. What you must know is that everyone must change at some point. Unfortunately for some, change can be death, but change must come. For others, it happens when the law takes away their freedom, and now you can mentally think about your decisions while sitting in jail.

This experience of being physically contained (jail) will always have you to sit yourself down and figure out the reasons behind your erratic behavior. *Then you will have an ear to listen to what you once refused to listen to.*

It is also a big problem if you never find yourself reasoning within yourself. Your mind will sometimes manipulate you into thinking that you want get caught if you are involved in criminal activities. Perhaps you've done it before didn't get caught and now you're rolling the dice on your own terms. For some, it is reason enough to change after getting away with something they should be doing jail time for, but for others, the only way they will change is when their criminal activities become painful to their emotional being, and this pain is felt only when some are confined and have a loss of freedom to roam where they so desire.

One of my former mentees whom I will call Don displayed a classic example of not knowing "self". He lost himself in the other guys because he needed them to validate who he was as a young man. Well, not only did they validate who Don was, but they all gave Don up during interrogation time carried out by the detectives. Like many, they gladly ratted on Don in order to receive a lighter prison sentence. The lighter sentence was 20 years in jail.

The story went like this. I was approached by Don's mom and ask to mentor him. A short time afterwards, Don and I had a brief meeting about how things will be and some small expectations I expected to see in his character. Well, Don agreed. A short time after working with Don for about a month and a half, I notice that he started to pull away. The one thing I always remain true to when mentoring young men is this. If they want my mentorship, I'll gladly work with them. If they don't have any desire for me to mentor them, that's ok too. I never push anything they don't desire, because it then becomes time wasted.

Soon after, Don's mom came to me and informed

me that Don had been hanging around the wrong guys. I approached Don on this issue, and he did not deny the story. Don had quit his job at a fast food restaurant and commenced to hanging on the street corner with the fellas. I asked him why did he quit his job and he stated," I don't make enough money at McDonalds". I then asked. How much money does a sixteen year old need to make while in school. He didn't answer so I assumed he had no answer. From that day forward he dodged me until he got caught along with his buddies for arm robbery. He and the fellas had robbed at least three gas stations. The rest of the story speaks for itself and the moral of the story is this. If you show me your friends I can help you see your future. It's not about judging someone on their looks, or who they chose to hang with, but it is more about their attitude, character, and who not to hang with that determines the pathway of young black males. *Never allow yourself to be cultivated by crime.*

Don ended up being sentenced to 20 years in prison at the tender age of 17. Because he took a plea bargain, this sentencing was actually lighter than the 60 years of imprisonment he was looking at, had he not taken a plea bargain.

The Understanding of Philosophy, Purpose and the Penal System

There are three important issues every young man should recognize during his walk in life. These three issues are either what many young black boys refuse to acknowledge, refuse to accept, or have no clue in knowing what either one could mean during their life time. Understanding the truth behind philosophy, purpose and the penal system will provide the basic foundation of how one deals with the issues they are faced with in life, and how one can better strengthen their character during their lifetime.

According to many philosophers, philosophy means to be in search of the truth. In my humble opinion, I perceive Jesus to be the way, the truth, and the light. By recognizing this, I have discovered the truth and it is the number one order in my life. Underneath this order is me and the positive things I decide to place within myself for the improvement of myself. If I refuse to search and understand the truth about me, then I am limited to my surroundings and unknowledgeable about me as an individual.

Too many young men have died senselessly secondary to the lack of understanding who they were before realizing what they could have become. The fact that many young men overlook this important detail in life becomes the reason why many continue to fail. The reason for their failure is due to the truth they may have never known about themselves and the rapid discovery of trouble when delving into a lifestyle that has a quick end. This is followed by the price they pay while trying to discover it.

On a different level, the challenge is not the streets or the hood when analyzing truth. The challenge is not someone moving onto your territory (which isn't own by you), nor is the challenge about making yourself seem bigger to other guys on a street level. The challenge deals with you. Once you realize this challenge, it is then up to you to rise above it. For example, how often do you challenge yourself in making good grades in school? Do you challenge yourself to walk in good character? Do you challenge yourself to search for those positive traits found on the inside, and use them as weapons while walking through life? Do you challenge yourself not to curse, not to smoke or drink? These are examples of a few challenges you should be indulging into if you are to create a better you.

The contrast to creating a positive character is accepting a negative surrounding. Many young black men have conditioned their minds to defend themselves against others that are usually enduring the same struggle but have an affinity to annihilate those who are perceived to be a threat. In truth, you will never win a battle and walk away in victory if you decide to couple with negative issues in the streets.

Why? Because, those issues that are in the streets will always remain issues of the streets as long as individuals dwell with a low mind and live with no purpose. Fighting with environmental issues by way of remaining a part of the problem will only lead to the paralysis of your character, self dilapidation, and an environment that loses value socially and morally.

Regardless of what your friends or others may say or try to become, it is true that every young man who is trying to be nothing, will ultimately become nothing. The reason is simple. Nothing from nothing can only produce a lifestyle which leads to nothing. The reverse side of this is, something from something, will only produce a lifestyle that will produce something.

Looking at this from a different angle introduces circumstances that are found on the streets and negative experiences that will always stand in front of you. If you are to strengthen and create better character for yourself, then elevating yourself to higher standards will only strengthen those potentials found on the inside and not battle with circumstances dwelling on the streets. You are the one that must change, if there is to be a change. The reason is this. Circumstances come and go leaving you to acknowledge that the only way to defeat that which is "negative" is to move rapidly towards a proactive lifestyle.

When you desire the change and have the strength to stand up as a young man, then elevating your mind will help you overcome negative circumstances. When your mind is elevated then growth in your character rise high enough to overcome your circumstances. By overcoming your circumstances it will move you from a lowly state of mind to a higher state of mind.

Elevating your state of mind will also introduce you to self acknowledgement. When you come to grips with self acknowledgement and self actualization, you will have reached the discovery point of knowing who you are, what you stand for and your reason for being. Having done this is like exercising the inner will, because now you have higher expectations of yourself and not what others expect you to be out in the streets.

It is unfortunate that many young men abort these gifts because they rather take a pathway that does not require much thought and intellect. In other words, it is easier to be nothing. And after years of being nothing, it becomes much difficult to arise from nothing, to become a part of a world that has always offered everything.

Furthermore, understanding "self" will involve acknowledging your state of mind and perception. If your mind and perception becomes distorted because of what you entrain and what you are exposed to, it will ultimately play a part in shaping your character as you dress and walk to what you feel you're deserving of for that moment.

In other words, it is easier to act like a thug, or dwell in ignorance because it pacifies the failures you are dealing with for that moment. In the end, when you are responsible for fathering two or three babies in this world, who looks like you, acts like you, and walks like you, it then becomes much difficult to effectively teach your kids the things in which you yourself decided to ignore in life.

Continuing, when we witness young black men walk around in a self degrading state, they are unaware that it pushes people away from acknowledging that piece of gold that can be found on the inside. The only attractions they may garner are those that have a similar mindset. This is why thugs and want to be thugs have issues with each other. A lowly state of mind can rarely rise above the other low mind because they each have a stronger reason for their existence, but in a low place in life.

They all have a kindred spirit and a similar mindset which in return have a greater affinity in competing to superimpose one another. The fight becomes one familiar spirit against the other. This result in young men that may have great potentials, but have disregarded their self worth and put themselves in a position to be captured and controlled. *Remember angry spirits can only identify and spark controversy with similar spirits because they can only identify with what they have failed to create within that moment of time.*

Whenever I am out and about, I constantly witness young men walking around with a chip on their shoulders for no reason at all. It appears to be the case secondary to the expressions that many have on their face and the anger many embody. This type of ignorance was once implanted in me so it is easy for me to recognize it. This is where many things are falsified concerning the philosophical being of young men who are lost. Many don't realize the price that was paid nor does he realize his own character of truth.

When he is at this stage in life, he is really not in search of himself, but he is on the run in preventing true self discovery of his abilities. His time is usually spent trying to figure other young men out and this lack of focus leads to becoming a follower by sagging, and wanting to be what he is not. Without a shadow of a doubt, he is essentially lost but feels the need to display a sense of coolness in order to get others to identify a strength which is really an inner weakness.

Some say it is simply a fad without giving thought to the lowly mindset and esteem that it creates over a period of time. In my opinion, I reference it as being a big weakness that camouflages the individual's true potentials. When young men fail to correct their weakness it leads to difficult consequences such as the lack of higher education, and the misunderstanding of self worth.

Some of the issues that follow in cases like these will fall along the sidelines of anger, loss of love, low self esteem or low self worth. Those that have a different walk in life (or higher mindset) understands the meaning of removing "self" from negative situations and understanding the ability to stand alone, even if others "hate" on them for doing so.

As a young man, when you can stand alone (especially when standing for the right) this is where the experience of strengthening will be found. Once it is discovered you will easily identify with yourself, instead of allowing negative attachments to identify who you are. In the end, others will notice and your character will present itself way before words can ever explain the truth.

Another fork in the road that many young men never discover is this: When young men place themselves in the pathway of dire situations and negative challenges, they usually have great fear in trying to achieve that positive experience. This happens because others that are negatively challenging them (or trying to convince them to do wrong) also fail to acknowledge their own self worth. This brings about a constant storm of negative issues. In other cases it will involve the male closest to you. All the while he may envy you all because he can see the strength in you, but will always fail to recognize it within his own self.

Without acknowledgement, it will soon oppose acknowledging what others are worth before the recognition of "self". The end result is the disrespect of something or someone else.

Ultimately, your life can only be lived out by you and your walk along the pathway in this world can only be walked by you. Your decisions on whether or not you should commit an act of crime or not commit it, is all up to you. This is the basic level of under-standing what the central part of "self" is all about. If you never decide to walk on a positive pathway during your inward walk of life, then you will find yourself making a whole lot of pit stops at the expense of the wrong you invited into your life. These pit stops can be considered to be areas such as jail, prison, probation courts, baby mamma drama, negative friends, or even death.

Overall, when you walk into unforeseen circum-stances the change may be difficult, but you still have the ability to think! Even though the truth can be painful you must first recognize your weaknesses if you are to regain your strength and move onward to the next positive pathway of life.

Case: *I knew another young man that was involved in a bank robbery by way of the window at the bank. After I spoke with him concerning the incident, he felt that he was innocent. I ask him if he knew the guy that he was riding with and he replied, "yes". He was the passenger in the car, while his associate committed the crime. This is my point: The young man professing his innocence not only knew that the driver was troubled but he also knew that the driver had a gun, which is a felony charge, right? My question to the guy professing his innocence was this. Why were you in the car with him if you knew he had a rap sheet of getting in trouble? Why didn't you get out the car once he pulled the gun on the teller? His answer: " I don't know. The* guy had already shot someone that previous week so I was scared." If this young man could go back and relive how he handled this situation, I'm sure it would be different. His biggest enemy was himself, and moreover, he failed to just THINK.

For many, this is where the door opens up for you to review the experiences of those you may have known or read about in the newspaper, or even seen on the evening news. Without a shadow of a doubt, if you refuse to learn of the consequences of those that have failed before you, then, your failure to open your eyes will soon become the very reason you will one day discover hope and believe.

Knowing Your Purpose

Lacking purpose is synonymous to disregarding life. If your purpose in life is to go nowhere in life, then, why would you ever take a stand? christopher

When you identify with the truth concerning yourself, it will open up the doors to your purpose in life. Your purpose in life is that element in your life that reminds you of what your walk in life really entails. Having a true purpose in life will strategically outline you as a person, as you place goals along the pathways you are traveling with the certainty, that you will reach a productive destination. Not having a purpose is not living at all.

Purpose can also be defined as that self- recognized inner drive that is identified by the way you respond to the challenges you're confronted with. In other words, your purpose is a reminder of the journey you started, and while traveling this mental GPS system lets you know the mileage to your destination. During your travel this system will also hold you accountable for the "good" you embark upon, and the "mistakes" you create.

So on, if you have no purpose it becomes difficult to hold yourself accountable for anything. This leads to acknowledging that the time you may have traveled can be considered wasted time. Contrast to this, if you ignore your purpose, then your reason for being what you never attempt to become would be considered purpose less.

Furthermore, having purpose allows you to seize the moment and dress up your inner gifts especially if you wish to adhere to the experiences of life that will move you forward. With that being said, young black males don't have to go to prison in order to discover their purpose nor a creative experience in life.

But without purpose, those inner desires you give in to will cause others to exploit your weakness causing you to express outer anger.

Experiences like these will place a systematical red stamp on your life and put you in a position to be controlled, *not by what others have done to you, but by the mistakes in which you brought* unto yourself. And for the ones that can easily say, "I don't care, or I'm going to do want I want to do" and still involve themselves in various crimes, they are the kind of guys that seek to be controlled because of failed knowledge and self desecration.

Although we all have gifts on the inside of us many people don't understand the purpose of their gifts because they never open their minds to acknowledging what they stand for in life. Having said that, if you never open up your mind to realize your purpose, then your abilities and gifts that are on the inside of you will never give you the chance to respond to what is never activated.

This is another example of how black men destroy themselves, before they get the chance to create themselves. It is not a conspiracy to bring the black males down, but on the part of the individual himself, it becomes a form of selfishness. Walking without a purpose blinds the true gifts that exist, but character weakness will always deny it.

The young man that is running with his buddies throughout the night, and hanging in areas he shouldn't be in *"is essentially destroying himself, before he makes himself."* This is how the transformation starts. There is no purpose in chillin, getting high or getting drunk. This simply denotes that you are destroying yourself characteristically when you hang with friends that expressive negative lifestyle like the aforementioned.

When negative attachments are in place it blinds your purpose, and when this is done young men then look for a reason to justify their failures. The one thing that prevents many young men from identifying with themselves when this occurs is the experience of fear. This emotional attachment of fear prevents you from acknowledging the experiences you connect with and have you believing that you must act "this way" in order to gain respect. At best, this is known as self manipulation and many black males are serving time behind bars because they could never push aside their fear. Instead they gambled with placing themselves in bondage.

When one is on the pathway of destruction involving "self" they can easily overlook that which has always stood right in front of them. The reason that positive opportunities can be overlooked lies within the expectations that you will have of yourself. When you don't expect anything of yourself, then, you will lack the ability to care about others. This is how boys somehow take on their "homeboys" attitude and mindset, when they seek to get their worthless approval.

You may never consider it "fear" because they are your homeboys. But in reality, your character growth is predicated upon your inner circle of friends and without doubt, negative friends will always obstruct your movement forward.

Next, you can easily tear down your purpose without ever realizing how great of an asset you are to the world. This is why "homeboys" without a purpose would say, "man, you have changed from how you use to be". The sad part is this. When changing from a person of good character to a person of bad character, the last one to realize that change is the "changed" individual. And like so many youths I have come in contact with, many of those that refuse to change don't realize how much the family is needed until they need them to bond them out of jail, or hire an attorney (out of the money they work hard for) to protect the very ones that have been unappreciative. This is not having a purpose in life. This is a choice that one makes and the consequences are what can reintroduce them back onto the track of true purpose.

There are many other reasons why young men fail to realize their purpose. Another one relates to self detainment. Young boys are notorious for detaining themselves from sprouting mentally because they inadvertently allow what they indulge in, to hold them hostage. When young men are held hostage, they are held hostage in a way that appears to be cool or a nature of habit by most. But in the end, expressing their coolness over the failure to educate their mind is detrimental for the soul and the spirit.

Webs of issues like these can overlap purpose and in many cases cause others to end up in a delusional state of mind because they made the wrong choices. From this delusional state of mind something crazy occurs, and then remorse is felt by "you" the assailant. In the end the family members that once believed in you are now struggling to right the wrong in which you created.

During the month of December 2010, I had the pleasure of speaking with a young man whom I would call Trey. Trey was not a bad young man, but like so many others, Trey liked hanging with guys that thought they were "hard." To make a long story short, Trey found himself hanging with several other young men, when they came across someone they had beef with. The nature of the problem is not the case. But because Trey was with the wrong guys, when a shooting occurred, Trey was also sent to jail and charged with attempted murder. There is a saying that goes. "What you don't know, can sometimes destroy you." Hanging with the wrong guys finally caught up with Trey, and because he was part of the pack, he is guilty by association, and the possibility of spending time in prison along with his boys became very real.

When young men find themselves involved in crimes like this, the majority of cases involve two or more people. This is also an example of how friends allow each other to hold themselves hostage to ignorance and unlearned behavior. With a case like this one, Trey went along for the ride because he failed to take a stand to protect his self worth, and his inner assets. He allowed himself to become a hostage, and now he will pay for it for the rest of his life.

Being taken hostage in the way of hanging with the wrong guys also exposes an inner weakness that lures you away from your true purpose. If you are hanging with the wrong guys, you will never have inner strength no matter how much you try to manipulate yourself. Why? Because your inner weakness is never strong enough to stand alone and therefore you seeks other weak minds that have common interest, to validate who you are.

At some point, you must realize that what you see as strength by hanging with negative friends, are really big signs of weakness. In other words, they (friends) are all weak collectively, but they look to each other for a strength that is artificial. *This type of strength never last because it is really a source of weakness that is seeking to appear strong.*

I have become a big fan of the television series, the First 48 hours. This is a real life homicide show that tells of the crime that has occurred in the past involving murder. Not to my surprise many of the victims are young black men that are killed senselessly. These detectives are usually able to solve the crime or at least get a good lead on the murder based on the type of crime. Usually the person that commits the crime has a history of committing crimes at some levels. In other words, they've made committing crime their purpose. The reason many of them commit the crime is because of exposure from their surroundings. In all realness, I don't think people grow up dwelling on how they are going to kill someone, only to be sent to jail, right? But, if you lack ambition and self worth, you will cultivate your lifestyle to that environment. This cultivation can manipulate you to believe that your survival depends upon doing wrong just to get ahead. This is when purpose is lost. *Sometimes what we claim our environment to be (the hood) is the very thing we should be denying ourselves the attachment towards.*

Sadly enough, when I go back to my neighborhood to visit, I still see some of the same people with the same mind set. Unfortunately, there are those that have died at early ages, and those that are still hanging around the neighborhood. Why, because they lost their purpose. Those that are still living there continue to neglect or identify with their purpose, and are beaten down by life with the use of drugs, alcohol, or some other negative proclivity they involve themselves in.

Moreover, some have even found their purpose in drinking, robbing, selling, or becoming a habitual offender. Unless there is a change made unto their minds and lifestyle, this is what will ultimately destroy them.

As a young man growing up in my neighborhood, it was hard to see in older men, what I can easily see now. The reason it is so visible now is because of the change I allowed myself to take on. Many of them had no purpose in life even back then. I attached myself to older guys that had no sense of purpose, because I was never aware or taught otherwise. We all felt it was cool to hang out, drink, and smoke. It was a lifestyle that was easy to perform and through my performances, I became attached to what felt good temporarily. It wasn't until I woke up and stepped onto the train of purpose that I realized the meaning of ME. Now, when I look back over the past, I realize that many of my child hood friends were destroyed because they never challenged their own ambitions nor recognized their true purpose. Failing to challenge your ambitions will lead you to barriers that lie within the pathway of your life, and as long as there are restrictive, your purpose will never be discovered.

Along the same lines of ambitions is the destination call discovery. *You must discover yourself if you wish to grow within yourself.* When in search of purpose, you will discover the truth about how you should approach society, and not how you should *owe your time to society* by spending time in jail. Your purpose should be the results of what you're striving for in life now, which leads to what the future will hold for you later. When you deny your character and embrace those things that will destroy you, the sufferings in which you will endure will be the suffering you would have chosen to endure.

As mentioned before, purpose can be seen as that experience kept in the fore front of your senses on a regular basis. If you sit back and think about hustling for the next dollar, then your purpose is falsified. Your purpose in life should always birth a meaningful end once you acknowledge it, and begin walking towards it. It is important to walk towards your purpose in life because it's an experience you must grow into if you're looking for change, and only movement brings about change. So, don't ever be fearful of change if there is failure, because failing a task can always be rewritten as conquering a task.

If you fall away from striving towards what you have the ability to become, you will find yourself walking along the interchanges of negativity. On the other hand, when you highlight your desires you will always grant yourself the ability to find confident in knowing that your purpose is not carried out nor created by anyone else other than yourself. Think about it. Would you do some of the things you've done if the influence of your friends were not involved?

Overall, if you remain blind to your purpose in life, your desires will never arrive at your destination without you in tow. If you find yourself fighting, selling drugs, planning to rob or engaging in other crazy things, then your true purpose in life will have been minimized and you will become divided against no one else but yourself. You may never understand how this division occurred especially if you are running the streets with others that are on the same level you are on.

The struggle to move from being a thug or weed head (which is not purposeful) to becoming a person with purpose is truly a small battle once recognition is acknowledge.

If you establish a connection to things such as weed smoking, robbing, stealing, and other crimes, you unknowingly establish connections with weaknesses. When such weaknesses like these penetrate your life, it obscures your purpose and only feed that emotional weakness for the time being. Why is this? This happens when one learns to rely on those things that are satisfying them for *the moment.* Creating your life off of a "moment" of good feeling, denies you the right to pull the best out of yourself.

Overall, when it is all said and done, every weakness you have in your life, will never attach itself to a stronger part in you unless you eliminate those weaker parts, in which are attached to you. In other words, discover your purpose and walk in your potentials.

The Penal System

When a young man refuse to take control of his own life, then Confinement becomes a place where he is surely to be controlled. CS

Imagine this. You are sent to prison and your physical freedom is taken away. You are told when to go to bed and when to wake up each day and night. Your cell phone is gone, the house phone is gone and the car you use to drive are all gone. When you feel the urge to run down the street and pick up something to eat, you can't. When you feel like walking out of your room to get something to drink, you can't. The privacy to use the bathroom is gone, and most of all, when you desire to see your family, they must all sign forms (hoping they don't have prior felony charges) and request to see you, because the freedom you once knew is gone!

All of these experiences and many more are natural experiences that we all take for granted and are never realized until they are taken away. The reason you can't do what seems natural is because you are sentenced to stay within the confinements of a jail cell to protect others from what you fail to acknowledge and protect about yourself. This is called freedom.

The freedom you once knew has now been placed

on hold until your debt to society is repaid. Without doubt, by trading in your freedom and adhering to a confined and lonely experience, you then become a statistic along with many others, and are left to figure out just who you are, and why you did it. In other words, *that in which you were born into (freedom) has now become limited, as freedom removes itself from a host it once knew.*

Going to jail means no physical freedom and no physical freedom equates to giving up your rights so that others may control you. Many young men that are uninformed see it as a conspiracy to get rid of black youths. I visualize it for what it is. The truth is, if you are involved in any type of crime that places your neighbor or environment at risk, then you are guilty of not understanding freedom and the price you pay is found behind the bars of the penal system.

When I meet young men that have been in and out of jail, I always like to present this simple question. If you had a choice and slavery still existed, would you voluntarily work on the plantation? Every last young man I have asked this question, have said they would never work on anybody's plantation. "No way," they would say.

Their answers are always surprising, but their actions are contradictory especially when many choose to live a life that will lead them onto a plantation like setting which is the prison. You may ask, how is it contradictory? Well, during the time of slavery, a man was only considered a slave when he allowed his mind to become defeated secondary to the conditions he lived in. Slavery was implemented as a way of control over the mind, while the physical body was subjected to cruel and unusual punishment. The word slave was superimposed upon them, not by way of the slaves, but by the master. In other words, anything that controls your mind ultimately controls you!

Many servants disliked the word "slavery" because the word slavery is really a mindset that a person takes on when they fail to acknowledge the harsh experiences that are presented before them. It is no secret that slaves were defeated before they could be made (into men) and the freedom they longed for was only a fragment of their imagination. Those that were servants of the past lived and worked on plantations because they did not have a choice and they were made to do what they wanted to refuse. But today, black men have a choice and too many of them are choosing to be reduced as men and controlled as subjects or prisoners

With the many black males that are piling up the prisons in our society today, it is a tragedy that many of them are not educated on what prison life is and the problems it impose upon their life after their time is serve. This is the classical example of people perishing because of a lack of knowledge. Many males are so dominant and egotistical, that they forget to understand the one thing that will propel them further throughout this pathway of an experience. That is self preservation of their own life.

Furthermore, there are many things we can do in our lives that will confine us to such a place. As of now, young black males populate the prisons more than any other ethnic group. The prison system has become a revolving door for many black youths that are too unfamiliar with the legal process, too naïve to stay away from criminal activities, and are too out of touch with their own purpose.

Similarly, when one dwells outside the realm of knowledge and misunderstand their purpose for living, it allows law makers to decide their fate when they are caught up in the web of crime. Some call it a tragedy, I call it the continued education of young black youths, because once you are imprisoned, you will then use the best of "you" to fulfill your potentials.

Alongside this statement, many prison systems have traded in their gloves of bringing forth justice, and are now looking for profit by incarcerating prisoners. Many of them are black males. In other words, many of the prisoners whom are bringing forth an increasing amount of wealth for prison investors are those that have chosen not to change nor deter from crime. I must say that I agree with Michelle Alexander and her book "The New Jim Crow." The war on drugs does seem to target the poor black communities, but does this excuse black men from being accountable and holding themselves responsible for black crime and murders.

Without doubt, it is very disheartening to walk into the inner city streets in which I know well and feel the threat of being robbed or killed by people I am accustomed to being around. The threat or fear doesn't go away. If young criminals were not arrested for the crimes that are done, what would living in the projects or other drug infested neighborhoods be like, with young dealers controlling these neighborhoods?

Needless to say, at the end of the day, one must ask the question that stands in front of the problem. Who are the ones doing the crime that places them within the revolving doors of the prison system? This is the only answer that truly matters. Once this answer is recognized by the individual that subjects himself to being sentenced, then, the prison industry will not profit off of the mistakes that are made so easily by the hands of black men. The problem want resolve itself, if black youths aren't arrested for drugs, robbery or murder. It will only escalate.

Secondly, young black males that are displaced and are creating havoc throughout different communities have long been the problem in which more positive and educated black males refuse to confront on a consistent basis. By continuing to not confront nor develop stronger relations within our young black males, it will only exacerbate the issues confronting the communities within our cities and those within close proximity will always share a hostile place with young men that vulnerable to crime. It is not only obvious that black males are refusing to be educated, have a higher affinity for crime and are having kids and leaving them behind, but many are also misunderstanding the concept of the their actions and the price that has to be paid.

I believe that any and all men that find themselves doing the crime, should ultimately do the time. This is a very simple concept, but it becomes more complicated when racial disparity is involved. It may be true that blacks spend more time for robbery etc., but this is irrelevant when it comes down to doing the crime. The question then becomes, why did you involve yourself with the crime? Why rob or kill anyone at all, when you know that imprisonment is the consequence you will have to face? Why sell crack or marijuana when know that going to jail is the consequence? The only rationale this suggest is that too many black men are not only lacking control of their own destiny, but they gamble at the chance of making quick money. This gamble leads to a tougher struggle after a felony charge is documented on your record.

Onward, I'm not going to touch on how much time a prisoner is given or why the prison systems should not profit off prisoners. I would like for my point to be directed towards each individual black male that finds himself in a position to commit a crime, and not realize that with committing a crime you must also realize that you must do the time.

With that being said, one must understand that selling drugs or being involved in criminal activities is one of the easiest jobs to hold, but it is the quickest way to limit your upward social mobility in society. If you think about it, the only reason drug dealers or gang bangers sell drugs or commit crime is all secondary to self profit or self satisfaction. This isn't how one should start their lives. This is nothing more than an act of selfishness by uprising off of someone that maybe experiencing a weak moment during their own life experience.

To say the least, the prison system as a whole is no different. To view it differently, the fight against why prisons should not profit from crime, is truly irrelevant, when in truth, black men should not easily give themselves over to becoming a liability, especially when you become viewed as a profitable asset for the prison to own.

So with that being said, how is it that young black men continue to find themselves trapped in this world wind of entanglement which has become an investment opportunity for many on Wall Street? Many young black youths become entrapped in such a web of crime, because they seemingly embark upon the wrong pathway early on and their lack of education makes them vulnerable to delving into other negative experiences that holds them hostage to their own ignorance. If you are looking to change, then start over by continuing the process of educating yourself to a higher level, and challenge yourself against the crimes you may have attached yourself to and ignore the vulnerable moments that may surround you.

For many, that vulnerability comes along when the untrained mind finds itself wanting to drop out of school, run with the wrong type of guys or simply commit a felonious offence. This is a pattern that I witness time after time and those that refuse to think rationally, will subject themselves to being confined physically. *In other words*: When you forfeit the game on education by way of higher learning, you also deny yourself the right to move upward as a productive citizen. In the end, a mind that does not move upward will either plateau or move downward because a lack of knowledge also leads to a vulnerable mind.

On a similar note, according to CCA (Correction Corporation of America), they are the fifth largest correctional facility in the United States. In many ways, this institution like others have found ways of success by housing unlearned minds. In part, what too many young black men fail to recognize about themselves before being sentenced into one of these institutions, is self worth. It is not just another black man going to prison, but it is more like "another brother denying

Moreover, CCA houses more than 75,000 prisoners in more than 60 facilities. Out of the 60 facilities there are 44 facilities that are privately owned. In other words, many of these beds within the private facilities are contracted out, and black males are making these prison beds their new home. There are no personal marketers that are sent out into the streets to invite these young black males into this institution. But one of the largest marketing tools that entraps recessive mind black men are discovered over the airways.

Through black music, many untrained minds of black youths find themselves trying to live out and create that in which they learn through negative lyrics. This is the tragedy.

The many black men that not only fail to recognize their self worth, or fail to see themselves as an asset, ultimately becomes a liability on the forefront of society by entertaining behaviors that leads them to the prison gates. After being arrested and placed into prisons, many are then moved from a state of being a liability in society to being used as an asset for corporate profit behind prison walls. This is a slave mentality that many black men themselves have created and have learned to use against none other than himself.

Next, how is it that black males become assets to prisons? Well, if you look at the type of work that is done within the prisons such as textile, clothing, production on mechanical parts, and others, black males are worked at cheap labor cost behind prison walls, and the prisons reap the benefits.

On average the prisoners are usually strong and able bodied men that are working to enhance bigger profits while receiving very little pay. Not only will the system work prisoners for cheap labor but they also provide an education, teach work ethics, and behavioral classes, for many of those that have a desire to be rehabilitated. But unfortunately, the recidivism rate of being returned to prison is over 70 percent which crushes the ideal of rehabilitation.

To say the least, being accountable is found within the hands of the individual. It is clearly obvious that the mistakes made by too many black males would become the reason why prisons are over populated and unless black males hold themselves accountable for the many crimes that lands them in prison, then one will always overlook the establishment of better character. This establishment highlights the negative issues concerning black youths and will pave the way towards the development of better character only if youths are willing to change.

All young men must realize that respect, education, work, and character build is an essential key to life. Once this is realized, self preservation will manifest itself in the most positive form possible.

Prison is not the answer, nor is prison the solution. Living a life of crime is not the answer, nor is it the solution neither. Knowing this is fundamental and the only person to blame for their mistakes prior to being sentenced into one of these facilities is the individual himself. So, before you take on negative attachments as you grow your character, take a measurement of yourself worth, and decide if you are more profitable inside of a prison cell, or outside of a prison cell.

If black youths continue to envision themselves as liabilities then companies with an invested interest will continue to profit from their blindness and their irresponsible actions. You shouldn't have to be sentenced to prison in order to understand "self worth."

Some may even ask, is this capitalism? Yes, this is capitalism at its' best, but I rather you understand the importance of educating yourself and positively moving forward in society, rather than imprisoning your mind by way of your actions.

One other thing to know is that you can be oppressed secondary to your conditions, but physical oppression should not drive you to mental regression. The optional pathway that will lead you into another direction is based on how YOU decide to educate yourself and market yourself in good character unto the world. Without having a clear mind about who you are as an individual places you in a predicament to be shifted secondary to a lack of substance.

This monopoly experience is more like a modern day plantation. The biggest difference aims at the men that are held captive at these prison sites. Unlike the old days of plantation slavery, many black males are selling themselves into the system when they conform to crime. When you fail to hold yourself accountable for the actions you perform, then social growth and good moral character will always be hard to come by. During the period of slavery, blacks were made to conform to things they resisted, but nowadays, black males put themselves on the block to be sold disregarding the price they have to pay.

Not only were slaves held captive on plantations against their will but there were laws that were implemented to break down their moral conscious and made them question their hope for freedom. In other words, it was unlawful to dwell outside of conditions other than being a slave for many of the servants. This is the mindset that many black males still carry on today. The only difference is that many of the males that are misguided are walking around with a theory that they have it together, but in reality they stroll around lost.

On the weekends during the times of slavery, slaves were given the opportunity to come together as a family (as much as they could) and there were even those that tried to find other family members that lived on different plantations. These plantations were seen as a place where servants were housed and controlled. This is similar to how the prison systems are ran today. Many families are still traveling to see their boys, and with great pride many mothers (especially) are in strong support of their sons know matter what they did. The only exception is that most prisoners that are being housed are there because they put themselves in situations and slaves were traded and sold for mere profit.

Just as the plantations were during the time of slavery, the prison system of the today is seen as a similar place that confines and control. Slave plantations were also a place where servants worked while profits went directly to a higher entity. Again, similar to plantations the prison system also confines and allow prisoners to work, but those products which are produced, never profit the prisoners they only profit bigger companies. So ask yourself, why would you be a slave?

Furthermore, when you fail to acknowledge and respect the boundaries within yourself it ultimately ends in someone controlling you. This kind of control usually occur secondary to the failure of acknowledging that which is given to "you" as an individual. If you never acknowledge that you must extend respect then you must understand that what you fail to give is what the system will fail to extend. That is RESPECT!

Respect will also garner knowledge along the way. Knowledge concerning yourself and the world around you is a needed gem that is overlooked way too many times. When young black men walk without knowledge they rarely interrogate their own character and rarely arrest the negative mannerisms found on the inside. I call this, calling attention to your own self issues.

This is an experience young black men should never overlook. If this is overlooked then others (the law) are now looking at you trying to decide in what jail they should place you and how much time you should receive.

Prison not only takes away your physical freedom but it challenges your mind to reach and think beyond a place in which you are made to stay (the jail cell). Consider this: When you start missing your family you have to make arrangements to see them. When holidays come around, you are still bound to the jail cell with hopes that you'll receive letters of encouragement before the holidays slip away. This type of treatment is synonymous to you staying within the confinements of your own room at home, but could never open the door to exit out. If you clearly don't understand what it feels like to go to jail, just lock yourself up in your room and deny yourself simple entertainments and do not exit your room at all for a period of three days.

On a different note, you must realize your own self worth before getting to the point of giving someone else the right to house your body under a controlled institution. Each moment that presents itself opens up a door of opportunity and gives you the chance to feel and experience freedom.

It is disheartening to know that when black males don't value themselves and their education, it opens a wider door to embrace negative experiences which lead to captivity.

Once you are behind bars the only sense of freedom you can express is mental freedom. If you are able to experience freedom both physically and mentally then why not live it outside of the jail rather than gamble with your chances of entering the penal system.

Continually, if you find yourself in prison or in jail for a length of time, it's usually an experience that you have already been through in your mind. The difference is this. You somehow manipulated yourself into thinking you couldn't be caught. But somewhere in your mind you knew of the consequences and that is why you took precaution in doing the crime. In other words, your passion to do wrong becomes the struggle.

This struggle conceals the truth concerning what you could be and somehow denies your mind the right to know what you shouldn't do. Somehow many choose to commit an act in which they felt committed to but being captured and incarcerated shines the reality upon the decisions you chose to ignore.

Other issues worth considering before your find yourself entering into the penal system, are the experiences you allow yourself to walk through. Notice I said, that you allow yourself to walk through. Each experience will always open up a door of opportunity and a chance to simply feel freedom. Maybe there was a time prior to jail or prison, in which you may have refused to work for a living. But now that you are in jail, you are hoping to get on work detail for the simple fact of feeling the freedom that picking up trash on the side of the roadway can bring you. No matter how you may deny it, you will find yourself struggling to feel that which you have always known.

Here is something else to think about. When you value yourself you invest in preserving everything that is good about yourself, right? You could never value yourself if you are involved in a life style that seeks to devalue your character. This is why the jails and prisons make so much money. If you think a whole lot of yourself then why would you sell drugs, gang bang, rob or commit any other act of crime when you know the consequences?

When you minimize the good traits about your character you put yourself into situations that challenge your freedom and reflect on your moral conscious. Overlooking situations like these often leads into an area of life that will always cause you to feel regret! For example, I never should have been in that car when that shooting occurred.

No matter how hard a person or organization strive to minimize crime throughout the world the ultimate decision reflects on the individual. If you want to raise the standards for your life you must start by removing yourself from all that is bad or evil. You as an individual must hold yourself accountable for the experiences that are before you because in the end, only you will deal with the consequences.

For many young men that walk without a sense of character and good attitude, being able to exercise freedom means nothing. It means nothing because they feel a sense of entitlement to do or say what they want to do or say without any consequences. What is missed from the equation of so many young men is their inability to understand their self worth and the unwillingness to utilize those things around them. If you stand divided against yourself and indulge in the negative things you commit to in life, then you will always be in denial of your true abilities. When you deny your abilities to come forward (such as doing your best in school, or other younger kids) you then start to dwell with a disability.

In the end, dwelling with the kind of disability I'm

speaking of locks down the mind and causes you (the individual) to work against yourself and others within your environment. If you free your mind away from the issues that seek to destroy you, it is only then that you will free yourself from what seeks to control you.

This ends the book on "The Noose on The Black Community."

15380808R00102

Made in the USA
Lexington, KY
24 May 2012